OUTSIDE OF THE GATEKEEPERS

ELIZA COLEMAN AT MONTICELLO

HUGH CARTER

 # Copyright Page

Outside of the Gatekeepers
Eliza Coleman at Monticello

Copyright © 2026 by Hugh Carter
All rights reserved.

This book is a work of historical reconstruction based on family history, archival research, and public records. While every effort has been made to ensure historical accuracy, some interpretations are presented in the context of limited or incomplete documentation.

Names, dates, and historical references are used in good faith for educational and scholarly purposes.

First Edition

isbn: 9798252763453
isbn: 9798253578582
isbn: 9798252751924

Published by:
Hugh Carter Publishing, LLC
United States of America

Printed in the United States of America

Cover design by ["ChatGPT / Hugh Carter Collaboration"]
Interior layout by [Hugh Carter]

For more information, contact: Hugh Carter Publishing LLC
P O Box 145 Beverly, NJ 08010-9998
hughlcarter.com

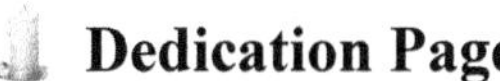 # Dedication Page

Dedicated to Eliza Coleman,
who stood at the gate when history looked past her,
and to the generations who carried her name,
her labor, and her memory forward—
even when the record did not.

This book is also dedicated to all those
whose lives shaped America
from just outside its most guarded doors.

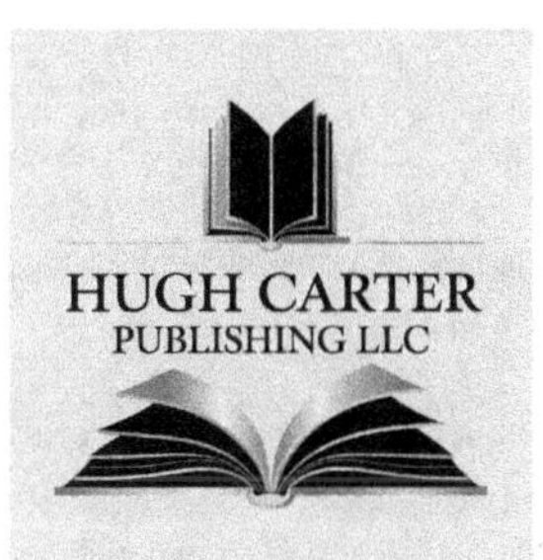

✒ Preface: At the Threshold

For much of American history, the story has been told from the inside.

The inside of houses.
The inside of power.
The inside of records and archives.

This book begins somewhere else—at the gate.

For more than forty years, my great-great-grandmother, Eliza Coleman, stood at the entrance to Monticello, the home of Thomas Jefferson. Her role placed her at a critical boundary: she controlled access to one of the most symbolically powerful estates in American history, yet her own life was never granted entry into the nation's official narrative.

This is not a traditional biography.
Nor is it a monument-centered history.

It is a family history shaped by proximity to power without access to it.

Like many African American families, ours inherited fragments—stories passed quietly, names partially remembered, roles acknowledged without documentation. The absence of records is not accidental; it is itself part of the historical design. What survives in the archive often reflects who was permitted to be seen, named, and preserved.

This book does not attempt to speak for the past, but rather from its margins.

By situating Eliza Coleman's life within the physical and symbolic space of the gate, this work examines labor, trust, surveillance, and silence during the early American republic. It asks how responsibility was assigned without recognition, and how entire lives could remain essential yet invisible.

To stand at the gate is to see both worlds at once.

This book is written from that vantage point.

— Hugh Carter

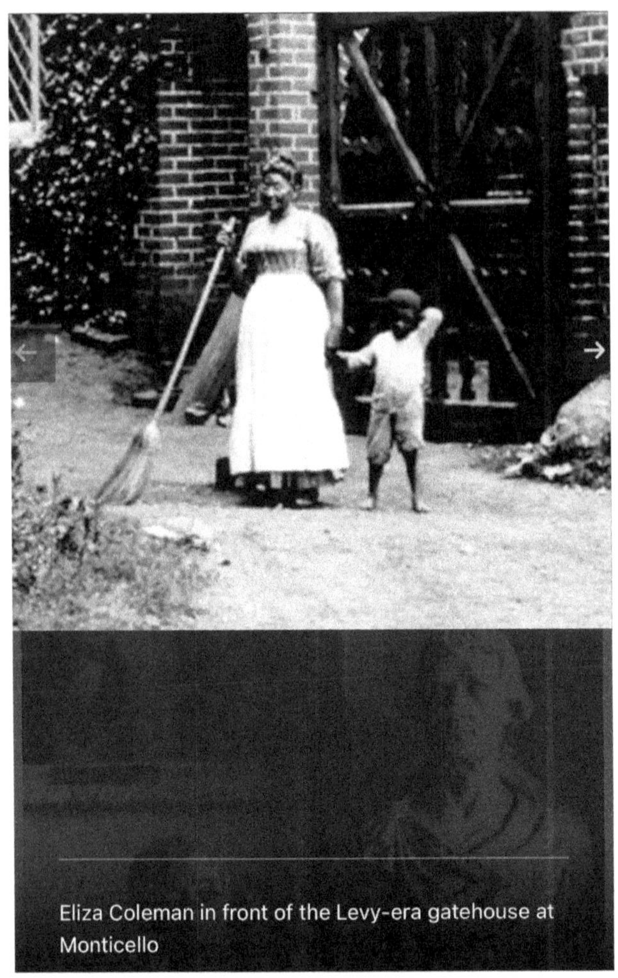

Eliza Tolliver Coleman

Chapter One — Outside of the Gate

The first impression of Monticello is not the house itself, but the approach. The road curves gradually upward, deliberately controlling sight and movement.

The estate reveals itself in stages, a design choice intended to establish order, hierarchy, and anticipation long before one reaches the main house.

At the threshold stood the gate.

The gate was not merely an architectural feature. It was a site of regulation, authority, and transition—a boundary separating public access from private power. For decades, that boundary was overseen by my great-great- grandmother, Eliza Coleman.

Her position as gatekeeper placed her at a critical point of contact between the world beyond the mountain and the carefully managed space above it. Every visitor passed through her presence. Every arrival was slowed, assessed, and directed. Yet her name rarely appears in the written narratives that describe the estate or its owner, Thomas Jefferson.

Eliza's labor was both visible and unacknowledged.

To stand at the gate was to witness history without authorship. She observed the rhythms of power—guests arriving, work beginning and ending, seasons changing— while remaining outside the authority those movements represented. Trust was placed in her role, but not extended to her voice.

What the historical record often omits, however, is that Eliza Coleman's life was not confined to her labor alone.

She was a wife and a mother.

Eliza married Thomas Coleman Jr., and together they formed a family with two daughters Lucy Coleman Barnaby Page and Grace Coleman Harris my great grandmother whose existence unfolded alongside the daily operations of Monticello. Their children were raised within the shadow of the estate—close enough to its structures to be shaped by them, yet distant from the privileges they symbolized.

Family life did not exist apart from labor; it was interwoven with it. Domestic bonds were formed and sustained under conditions defined by work, surveillance, and limited autonomy.

This dimension of Eliza's life complicates any attempt to reduce her to a single role. She was not only a gatekeeper in function, but a woman whose responsibilities extended beyond the threshold she guarded. Marriage and motherhood anchored her identity in continuity—through children who carried her name, her memory, and her presence forward even as the official record fell silent.

The gatehouse itself was small and utilitarian, intentionally modest. It was never meant to be admired. And yet it was one of the most consequential spaces on the property. It filtered movement, regulated access, and quietly enforced the social order of the estate.

Records preserve the architecture, the correspondence, and the visitors. They rarely preserve the interior lives of those whose labor sustained the system. Eliza Coleman appears in fragments—roles noted, functions implied—but not as a full historical subject.

Family memory fills where archives end.

In our family, Eliza was remembered through story rather than documentation. She "worked the gate." She "was trusted." She "raised children there." These statements carried meaning even without dates or formal records. They acknowledged presence where history often records absence.

This book does not claim to recover every detail of Eliza Coleman's life. It seeks instead to place her where she always stood —at the boundary between inclusion and erasure—and to recognize her not only as a laborer, but as a wife, a mother, and an ancestor.

The gate did not open both ways.

But life continued on both sides of it.

And this book begins there.

My first cousin Paul Clinton Harris, Esq.

Paul C. Harris, the former delegate for the 58th District, filled the seat in the Virginia legislature once held by Thomas Jefferson. Now Harris has discovered that his family has deep roots at Jefferson's home.

Paul Harris' **grandparents**, Rosa Harris and Joseph Harris, pose with his aunt, Louise Harris, in this 1928 family photo.

Unexpected ties to history

By Bob Gibson
Daily Progress staff writer

Five years after leaving the House of Delegates, former Del. Paul C. Harris is learning more about family roots that stretch back to slaves at Monticello at least as far as the middle of the 19th century.

Harris and one of his aunts, unofficial family historian Sylvia Coles, said they are convinced now more than ever that their family is descended from Thomas Jefferson's slaves.

Two Charlottesville authors, Monticello's Lucia "Cinder" Stanton and Henry S. Wiencek, who has uncovered new information about George Washington's slaves, said evidence linking Harris to an 1860s-era slave of a Monticello caretaker leaves open the possible tie of his family to the plantation home of Jefferson's time.

See **FAMILY** on **A9**

Harris and Coles accept the ties as far back as they are known with growing pride and curiosity. " It's an incredible story," Harris said. "The important research conducted at Monticello confirms that my family is an important stick in the American fabric. I am proud of my ancestors who helped grow, cultivate and preserve the Monticello that America know, love and cherish as their own."

Oral history catalogued

Stories that were handed down from one generation to the next are finding new historical context on Monticello's website, www.monticello.org where Harris recently said he discovered photographs and discussion of our family.

The text describes our family as having worked at the gatehouse on Route 53 as gatekeepers. For the extended family, "Monticello was home for almost two centuries, much longer than for anyone who held title to the property.""My jaw dropped" when he clicked on the Monticello's gatekeeper page of an oral history section, Harris said. Up popped a photograph of our maternal grandparents, Joseph and Rosa Harris, and a 1912 photo of Eliza Coleman, our great-great grandmother, standing in front of the gatehouse. Our grandfather "looked very proud, and he was very well-dressed. I just love that picture."

"Even today, our family are cooks [and caretakers] who pride themselves to be looking out for people." he said. "It's the mentality of a gatekeeper."

Coles, whose photo albums contain generations of ancestors at Jefferson's front gate a mile from where she and seven of her nine siblings were born, said family lore includes warm and vivid tales of playing around the gatehouse and on Monticello Mountain.

"We all used to go there because our aunt used to live up there at the gate. That was our playground all summer long," said Coles. "We always knew Thomas Jefferson was kin to us.

We were always told that." We called Thomas Jefferson 'Uncle Thomas,'"out of affection and perhaps kinship, she said. In the family's oral history, "we were always told Sally Hemings was one of our relatives."

One of her photo albums contains a May 23, 1955, Daily Progress with a story about the previous day's fire that destroyed the home where she was born and killed three members of her family. In that article, Mrs. J.H. Morris of 501 Park St. is quoted as saying the burned-out family of Joseph and Rosa Harris who had ten children in total. "are direct descendants of slaves at Monticello."

Morris was collecting clothing for the family, said Coles, who was employed at the home of Morris, whose first name was Rachel.

"Here's a white woman who knew our history, but we didn't know she knew."

Genealogy Investigated

Stanton, the Shannon senior historian at Monticello, said that since 1993 the Thomas Jefferson Foundation has interviewed almost 170 descendants and others who believe they are connected to Monticello. The research done so far into that history shows "there is a possibility of a connection to the Monticello of Jefferson's time, but we've been unable to pin it down or get farther back than the 1860s."

"Nevertheless, the Colemans were longtime residents of Monticello in the period of Levy ownership [between 1834 and 1923] and their descendants have wonderful memories of visiting them at the Monticello gatehouse," Stanton said. Monticello historians have been unable, so far, to establish a definite connection between Harris and slaves at Monticello owned by Jefferson, she said.

"We do know that Thomas and Eliza Coleman lived and worked at Monticello in the early years of the 2oth century," Stanton said. "And it seems highly probable that Thomas Coleman Sr. was the slave of Joel Wheeler, who was the caretaker of Monticello" from the period of the Civil War until 1878.

Sam Towler, has written about Monticello residents from 1853 to 1883, said the Thomas Coleman who married Eliza appears to be a grandson of Thomas Coleman Sr., a slave belonging to Wheeler, who prior to 1860 was overseer at Carter's Bridge for Benjamin Franklin Randolph, a grandson of Thomas Jefferson Towler a cousin of Wheeler's adopted son, said court records indicate that the man he believes to be a direct ancestor of my grandfather died at Monticello in 1888 at age 80 and could have lived there during the period before Jefferson died there on July 4, 1826.

On July 4, 1826, eighty-three-year-old Thomas Jefferson exhaled his final breath in the house he began constructing fifty-seven years earlier.

His only surviving child, Martha Jefferson Randolph, inherited the enormous debt her father had accrued as well as Monticello and its grounds—unmaintained for years due to lack of funds and in decline.

Martha Jefferson Randolph and her children continued living in the house after her father's passing. In need of cash, the Randolph family held an auction in 1827 for Jefferson's household and kitchen items, slaves, animals, and crops, but the sale's proceeds were insufficient to pay off Jefferson's $100,000-plus debt. Additional sales for Jefferson's personal possessions attracted little interest and did poorly.

"The Thomas Coleman born in 1808 ... must have lived on the grounds of Monticello, and the Thomas Coleman born in 1830 also," said Towler, whose mother's family had lived at Monticello during the Civil War. "My best guess is that the gatehouse was built in the 1850s," he said.

Wiencek, who has written two books about slave families in the 1800s and researched the lives of Jefferson's slaves, said that family oral history is a "very tricky source."

But, Wiencek believes, some of Paul Harris's direct ancestors not only were slaves at Monticello in the 1860s but that the Colemans at the gatehouse had American Indian ancestry - an opinion shared by Coles, my aunt.

"It's very plausible." said Wiencek, a member of the state Library Board. "We were Cherokee Indians," Coles said matter-of-factly.

Monticello appears as glad to welcome Harris into the history of Jefferson's home as the former delegate is to claim the ties. " I talked to Paul and he is so excited about it," said Daniel P. Jordan, president of the Thomas Jefferson Foundation, owners of the presidential home since a 1923 purchase from the Levy family that held the property for 89 years.

"What could be more exciting than to discover that an ancestor was part of history in a conspicuous way:" Jordan said.

"It's Monticello's goal to approach the past in the most accurate possible way, which means taking an inclusive approach," he said. "

Jefferson is front and center, but hundreds of other individuals, including an enslaved community, are important parts of the story."

What goes around ..,

Harris was elected to Jefferson's former seat in the House of Delegates in 1997 and re-elected in 1999. He was the first black Republican elected to the General Assembly in more than 100 years.

Harris resigned his seat in 2001 to work in the U.S. Justice Department. He is was senior counsel and director of enterprise compliance for Raytheon, a major U.S. defense contractor, in Arlington.

He said he has not given ups desire to run for statewide office someday. " My passion for politics still burns, but I'm at a point where I would have to make a very sober decision about what to do," Harris said.

My family and I continued to learn more about the family's long ties to Monticello and beyond. "It's been like a history lesson learning about the family." Anyone might do the same if family history referred to America's third President as "Uncle Thomas."

Eliza Tolliver Coleman

In the words of a descendant, Eliza Tolliver Coleman lived "up on the mountain all of her life." Members of her extended family lived and worked at Monticello over the course of a century—far longer than any of the property's owners. According to family tradition, Eliza Coleman "came out of that Thomas Jefferson tree," but her exact connection to Monticello's enslaved families is not yet known. She married Thomas Coleman born in 1808 (1845- post 1910), grandson of a former slave of Joel Wheeler, manager of Monticello during and after the Civil War. They had eight children.

Thomas Coleman was an ox-team driver and Eliza Coleman was gatekeeper for Jefferson Monroe Levy, owner of Monticello from 1879 to 1923. The position eventually passed to her daughter Lucy Coleman Barnaby Page (1869-1956), who was a midwife in the local community as well as the gatekeeper. Descendants have vivid memories of summers spent at the Monticello gatehouse.

Statement of Daniel P. Jordan, Ph.D.
DNA Press Conference at the International Center for Jefferson Studies November 1, 1998

In the Jeffersonian tradition, the Foundation welcomes new information and insights - We saw Dr. Foster's article in Nature for the first time less than forty - eight hours ago, and we'll need more time to evaluate it thoroughly. Meanwhile, we eagerly look forward to public discussion of the conclusion reached in the article and to evaluations of those conclusions by the scientific and historical communities. Dr. Foster's DNA evidence indicates a sexual relationship between Thomas Jefferson and Sally Hemings, an African - American woman who was one of his slaves. Slavery and race are uncomfortable subjects for many

**My Grandmother and Grandfather, Rosa and Joseph Harris Sr.
early 1900's**

Americans - but they are in the mainstream of our interpretation at
Monticello today precisely because they are part of the Monticello
story. The Foundation has long believed that you cannot understand
Thomas Jefferson without understanding slavery, and that you
cannot understand Monticello without understanding its African -
American community.

Further, we believe a scholarly approach is always key as we seek to advance our core mission of preservation and education. The Monticello staff includes Ph.D.'s as well as six individuals who have written one or more books with a university press. The Foundation has its own research center, which fields approximately 1,100 serious queries a year from the media, scholars, and other interested parties seeking accurate information about Thomas Jefferson and his times.

The Foundation will evaluate carefully Dr. Foster's findings and any other relevant evidence on the subject; and then, in the Jefferson tradition, the Foundation will follow truth wherever it may lead us.

The Thomas Jefferson-Sally Hemings controversy is now almost two - hundred years old, and it is one about which honorable people have disagreed. Few Americans have been more vigorous advocates of scientific pursuits than Jefferson. To reduce the mysteries of the past and move us all closer to the truth is in the spirit of Thomas Jefferson.

Bonds Form at Jefferson Bash Descendants of Slave Attend Gathering

Descendants of Thomas Jefferson's slave, Sally Hemings joined Jefferson's offspring at his plantation on Saturday, the first such meeting in 170 years. The families were at the annual gathering of the Monticello Association.

They promised to stay close, whether or not they become official blood cousins.

" I hope this is the beginning of a long relationship." said James Truscott, a white descendant of Jefferson's daughter Maria and vice president of the Jefferson family's Monticello Association.

Jefferson, who became president in 1801, was accused publicly in 1802 of being the father of several of Sally Hemings' children. Scholars have argued about the truth of the report ever since.

A DNA study that was published said Jefferson may have fathered at least one of Hemings' children.

On Sunday in a Charlottesville hotel, Truscott's nephew, Lucian Truscott, will challenge members of the association to admit the Hemings descendants and let them be buried at the family graveyard at Monticello.

But on a sunny afternoon on a majestic Blue Ridge mountaintop the atmosphere was cordial as relatives shook hands, exchanged family stories and in some cases addresses for Christmas card exchanges.

"We're still going to be family, regardless of what the Monticello Association does," Hemings descendant Shannon Lanier said. "We've always known it, since we were kids, that we were family."

Hours later, the families planned to drink and dine together at
a historic tavern down the road.

"I believe this weekend is about an opportunity for
individuals who share a common heritage and common ground at
Monticello to come together and to get to know one another better,"
Jefferson Foundation President Dan Jordan told the families.

The Hemings gathered together at the founding father's
plantation since Jan. 15, 1827, said Jordan, whose foundation runs
Monticello.

On that day, six months after Jefferson died deeply in debt,
130 plantation slaves from once over 600 plantation slaves and and
other possessions were sold at an auction. Shortly thereafter Sally
Hemings and five members of the Hemings family were freed.

"My kids will be reading about this in the history books" said Hemings descendant Troy Harding , of Chillicothe, Ohio, as he walked along Mulberry Row where Jefferson's slaves once lived.

The resemblances between the family members were remarkable. "You see facial features in them, and say, hey, you look just like my aunt," You can tell we're cousins."

They walked together beside Jefferson's European-style alcove bed covered with a crimson rose bedspread. They went through the underground stone passage way to Sally Hemings' tiny bedroom.

Jordan said the Jefferson-Hemings relationship "Is an American story," and Hemings descendant Shay Banks- Young of Columbus , Ohio, said it represents a chance to heal race relations.

"It's important begin mending bridges that broke down after generations and generations of slavery and segregation." she said.

Coleman & Henderson

Monticello was home to the Coleman and Henderson families for over a century, much longer than for anyone who held title to the property.

Beginning in the 1860s, generations of these families greeted visitors at the Monticello gate and gave tours of the house and grounds. They worked first for the Levy family, Monticello's owners from 1879 to 1923, as cooks, gardeners, ox team drivers, and household employees.

Eliza Coleman was Monticello's gatekeeper during the Levy era. According to family tradition, she "came out of that Jefferson tree," but her connection to Monticello's enslaved families is not yet known. Her husband, Thomas Coleman, was the former slave of Joel Wheeler, who managed Monticello during and after the Civil War.

Many Coleman descendants continue to live in Albemarle County. Eliza Coleman's great-great-grandson Paul Harris was elected to Thomas Jefferson's former seat in the House of Delegates in 1997 and again in 1999.

The Coleman family is linked by marriage to another family with long Monticello associations, from gatekeeper Willis Shelton to his grandson Willis Henderson, who was born at Monticello during the Levy ownership and worked for the family as a cook, waiter, and house guide.

After the early deaths of his parents Lizzie and William Shelton (both of whom were buried at Monticello), he and his sister Mary Elizabeth Henderson were taken to live in New York City with Jefferson Monroe Levy's sister, Amelia Levy Mayhoff. Henderson preferred Virginia to New York, and eventually returned to work at Monticello, staying on when the Thomas Jefferson Memorial Foundation assumed ownership of the property in 1923. He greeted visitors there through the 1960s, including Franklin and Eleanor Roosevelt.

By the way. The Monticello is just two miles north of my family's land in Simeon, Virginia. Slavery wasn't abolished in America until 1865 when the Thirteenth Amendment was ratified. Eliza started working the gate in 1879. We know that the Colemans were longtime residents of Monticello in the period of Levy ownership [between 1834 and 1923] and that Eliza got married to Thomas Coleman Jr. while living at the Monticello in 1845 before slavery was abolished. One could reasonably assume that Eliza was older than nine years old, before getting married and having eight children.

This places Eliza inside of the Monticello in close proximity to Thomas Jefferson and his family as a slave and then eventually as an employee. This is also within proximity of Sally Hemings in which the DNA has proven to be connected to Thomas Jefferson, Third President of the United States. Becoming a gatekeeper back then at this plantation was rare. My family believes that only Sally Hemings relatives were given this elite position back then and held it for over 100 years. My family also had land and a community.

Eliza Coleman and children at Monticello

Chapter Two — A House Seen From The Road

Many African American communities in Albemarle County formed near former plantation regions.

Because Rose Hill was near the region surrounding Monticello, it's possible that:

- some residents were descendants of enslaved people
- some were free Black families
- some migrated there after emancipation

These communities often existed in the shadow of major plantations but built their own independent institutions.

The road that climbs toward Monticello does not reveal the house all at once. Instead, the landscape stages the approach. The hill rises gradually, framed by trees that seem to guard the horizon, until the traveler reaches a point where the view opens and the structure appears— balanced, symmetrical, unmistakably deliberate. For generations, visitors have described that first glimpse as an encounter with American genius: the home of Thomas Jefferson, architect, statesman, and third president of the United States.

But for many people who lived and worked in its shadow, the house was not first encountered from the summit. It was seen from the road below.

From that lower vantage point, the building appeared less like a philosophical statement and more like a distant authority. The dome sat above the trees like a signal of power, visible long before the details of columns and brickwork came into focus.

To those approaching on foot, by wagon, or later by carriage, the house was something to be measured against distance. The road itself became a boundary between ordinary movement and controlled entry.

Before anyone reached the main house, they encountered the gate.

In the nineteenth century, the gates below Monticello were not merely ornamental. They marked the point where access shifted from open countryside to private domain. Beyond them stretched a carefully organized landscape of fields, orchards, workshops, and quarters—an entire working world that sustained the estate. And at that boundary stood a figure whose presence rarely appeared in official records but whose authority was unmistakable.

That figure was **Eliza Coleman**.

For more than forty years, Eliza occupied the role of gatekeeper at Monticello. Her position was both literal and symbolic. She stood at the threshold where travelers announced themselves, where deliveries were acknowledged, where strangers were measured and sometimes turned away.

She watched the road and the gatehouse with a vigilance that came from long familiarity. Over time, the rhythms of arrival and departure became part of her daily life.

From the perspective of historical narrative, this role is unusual. Histories of Monticello tend to begin at the house itself—its architecture, its gardens, its owner. Yet Eliza's story begins elsewhere. It begins at the edge of the property, where the road met the gate and where the view of the famous house remained distant but constant.

To understand that position is to understand something about the geography of power.

The approach to Monticello was designed to impress visitors. Jefferson's architecture embraced classical symmetry, and the surrounding landscape reflected enlightenment ideals about order and cultivation. Fields were arranged deliberately. Paths curved in ways that revealed and concealed views. Even the climb to the house was meant to shape perception.

But those designs were experienced differently depending on where a person stood.

From the portico of the house, the land spread outward like a carefully arranged map. From the gatehouse, the same land appeared as a place of work and vigilance. The road brought a steady procession of travelers—neighbors, merchants, curious visitors, and sometimes those whose business was less welcome. The gatekeeper had to read these movements and respond accordingly.

For Eliza Coleman, the gate was both workplace and vantage point. Family memory describes her as steady and observant, someone who understood that authority often lived in small gestures rather than grand declarations. A gate opened slowly could signal caution. A brief pause before answering a question could establish distance. Over decades, such moments accumulated into reputation.

Travelers who approached the gate would first see the small brick structure that guarded the entrance. Its architecture echoed the aesthetic of the larger estate but on a modest scale. A low wall extended outward, creating a sense of enclosure. Wooden doors marked the passage.Nearby stood the gatehouse itself—a building that was part residence, part checkpoint.

Nearby stood the gatehouse itself—a building that was part residence, part checkpoint.

From there, the road continued upward toward the hill.

On clear days, the dome of Monticello could be seen from the gate, rising above the trees like a reminder of where ultimate authority rested. Yet the physical act of entry remained in Eliza's hands. She stood at the point where decisions about movement were made. That responsibility, repeated daily over decades, gave her a role that was both practical and symbolic.

It is easy to overlook such positions in historical writing.

Grand narratives tend to focus on the architects of systems rather than those who maintained them. The documents preserved in archives often record property transactions, political correspondence, or architectural plans. They seldom dwell on the routines that kept an estate functioning day after day.

But those routines shaped the lived experience of Monticello as surely as the design of its dome.

Every delivery wagon that passed through the gate carried supplies needed by the household. Every visitor announced at the entrance set in motion a chain of communication that reached the house above. The gatekeeper stood at the center of these exchanges. In that sense, Eliza's role placed her at a crossroads of information and authority.

She saw who came and who left.

She observed patterns that others might miss.

And over time, she became part of the landscape itself— someone whose presence travelers expected when they approached the estate.

For those living nearby, the gatehouse served as a familiar landmark. Children growing up in the surrounding area would have known the place where the road narrowed and the brick walls appeared. Farmers bringing goods to the estate likely paused there before continuing up the hill. Visitors unfamiliar with the property would have encountered Eliza before seeing the house in full.

From the road, the scene carried a quiet drama.

Behind the gate lay one of the most famous homes in America. In front of it stretched the ordinary countryside of Albemarle County. The gatekeeper stood between these worlds, mediating their contact. Her position required patience, attentiveness, and a sense of responsibility that did not depend on public recognition.

It is precisely this kind of role that often disappears from the
historical record.

When historians describe Monticello, they frequently emphasize
Jefferson's intellectual vision or the architectural innovations that
distinguish the house. Such topics are undeniably important. Yet they
represent only part of the story. The estate functioned because many
individuals performed tasks that rarely entered written history.

Eliza Coleman's work belonged to that category.

Her presence at the gate reminds us that the estate's boundaries were
not abstract lines on a map. They were lived spaces where decisions
were made, questions were asked, and authority was exercised. The
gatekeeper was the person who embodied that authority on the
ground.

Seen from the road, Monticello was a distant promise of grandeur. Seen from the gatehouse, it was the destination toward which every visitor moved—but not always immediately.

Sometimes the gate remained closed.

Sometimes questions had to be answered.

Sometimes the road itself became a place of waiting.

In those moments, the gatekeeper's role became clear. She was the first human presence travelers encountered when they approached the estate, and often the last they saw when they departed. Her work shaped the rhythm of entry and exit, of permission and delay.

For more than four decades, Eliza Coleman stood in that position.

The house above the hill became famous across the nation. Visitors wrote about its architecture, its gardens, its connection to the founding of the republic. Yet the story of the gate remained largely unrecorded.

This book seeks to change that perspective.

To look at Monticello from the road is to shift the center of attention away from the summit and toward the boundary. It is to ask how power appeared to those who lived at its edges. And it is to recognize that history often unfolds in places where the official narrative rarely looks.

At the gate, the view of the house was constant but distant.

At the gate, the road brought the world to Eliza Coleman's door.

And from that vantage point—standing just outside the center of power—she watched history pass.

To understand the life of Eliza Coleman at Monticello, one must also confront the historical reality of the world in which she lived. During the years when Eliza stood watch at the gate, the estate was still shaped by the institution of slavery. The roads, buildings, gardens, and workshops that defined Monticello did not exist apart from that system; they were sustained by it. Life on the mountain included enslaved families whose labor formed the daily foundation of the plantation.

Eliza Coleman lived within that world.

Family history places her presence at Monticello during the late eighteenth and early nineteenth centuries, when the estate functioned not only as the residence of Thomas Jefferson but also as a working plantation. Hundreds of people—enslaved laborers, craftsmen, domestic workers, and their families—lived and worked on the property at different points during Jefferson's lifetime. Their lives unfolded in spaces that surrounded the main house: fields, outbuildings, workshops, and quarters scattered across the mountain.

It was within this environment that Eliza's life took shape.

Historical fragments suggest that she lived on the property for many years, eventually assuming responsibilities associated with the gatehouse. While the precise circumstances of how she came to occupy that position remain uncertain, the role itself was significant. The gatekeeper lived near the entrance to the estate, at the place where the public road met the boundary of the property. That location meant that Eliza's life was connected both to the inner workings of the plantation and to the world beyond it.

During her years at Monticello, Eliza married Thomas Coleman Jr. and they had eight children. One of her daughters Grace Coleman Harris was my great grandmother who married my great grandfather Henry" Papa " Harris and they had a son my grandfather Joseph Henry Harris who married Rosa Smith Harris and they had 10 children.

Thomas (Jr.) and Eliza Coleman (Our most removed ancestors for whom records can be located . They lived and worked at the Monticello in the early years of the twentieth century. The writer from The Daily Progress, Bob Gibson ran this story. That the lead researcher on the "Getting Word Oral History Project at Monticello. " It seems highly probable that Thomas

Coleman was the son of a slave Thomas Coleman Sr. who belonged to Joel Wheeler who was once the caretaker of Monticello.

Joel Wheeler was a caretaker of Monticello in the mid- nineteenth century. Before coming to Monticello, he was Benjamin Franklin Randolph's farm manager at Carter's bridge (Round Top) farm.

When Uriah Phillips Levy took possession of Monticello in 1836, Thomas Jefferson's estate was in less-than- pristine condition. Levy hired Wheeler, a local resident, to direct needed repairs and renovations. Levy – who resided at Monticello only for brief periods – and Wheeler are credited with doing a commendable job of restoring and maintaining the house and grounds over the next fifteen years.

Wheeler stayed on at Monticello after the outbreak of the Civil War in 1861 and Levy's death in 1862, and apparently became more cantankerous — and less concerned with upkeep — as the years unfolded. When Benjamin Franklin Ficklin purchased Monticello from the Confederate government in 1864, the property was in disrepair. "The place was once very pretty, but it has gone to ruin now," wrote a young woman who visited in the summer of that year.

"The parlor retains but little of its former elegance, the ballroom ... on the second floor has a thousand names scratched over the walls." Maintaining property in Virginia during and after the Civil War was difficult at best, but Monticello's decline in the 1860's.

Eliza had two daughters named Grace and Lucy. Her daughter Lucy Coleman Barnaby Page became the next gatekeeper in 1898 when Eliza had become too old. Apparently the elder Wheeler did not leave his estate to Joel Wheeler - the Monticello caretaker - as retribution for Joel Wheeler having set free a man in 1863 a slave named Thomas (last name unknown). This slave is believed by the historians to be Thomas Coleman Sr.] According to a deposition in the case.

Thomas himself had a history tied to the complicated networks of plantation life in Virginia. Family accounts identify him as a former enslaved man associated with Joel Wheeler, a local slaveholder whose name appears in records from the region surrounding Charlottesville and the rural communities of Albemarle County.

Like many individuals who lived in that era, Thomas's early life was shaped by conditions that limited personal autonomy and family stability.

Yet within those circumstances, families were formed, relationships endured, and communities developed. The marriage of Eliza and Thomas Coleman represents one such story.

Their union joined two individuals whose lives intersected with the broader structures of slavery while also expressing a personal commitment that transcended those constraints. Family memory holds that they built a household together at Monticello and raised children there. In doing so, they became part of the generational fabric that extended across the plantation landscape.

The presence of children added another dimension to life at the gatehouse.

A gatekeeper's residence was not an isolated outpost but a home. The rhythms of family life—meals prepared, children raised, conversations shared—unfolded alongside the responsibilities of guarding the entrance to the estate.

Travelers approaching the gate may have seen Eliza standing watch, but behind that public role existed the private life of a mother and wife whose days were shaped by family obligations as much as by duty. In this way, the gatehouse served as both workplace and household.

For Eliza's children, the road outside the gate would have been a constant presence. Wagons rolled past carrying supplies. Visitors arrived from nearby towns. News and rumors traveled along that same path. From the vantage point of the gatehouse, the outside world was always in motion, even while life within the estate followed its own routines.

My Grandmother Rosa Smith Harris, My Aunt Louise Harris, My Grandfather Joseph Henry Harris Sr. in 1928. Thank you!

Meanwhile, the house on the hill remained the center of authority.

Monticello's architecture reflected Jefferson's intellectual ambitions and his fascination with classical design. Yet the functioning of the estate depended on an entire community whose lives unfolded beyond the walls of the main residence. Artisans produced nails in the nailery workshops. Farmers worked the surrounding fields. Domestic workers maintained the household above.

And at the gate, Eliza Coleman watched the road.

Her role was not ceremonial. The gate represented a practical boundary that organized movement across the property. Deliveries, visitors, and messengers passed through under the observation of someone whose job required attentiveness and judgment.

Over time, that responsibility placed Eliza in a unique position within the social geography of Monticello.

Eliza Tolliver Coleman

She stood where the outside world met the plantation.

She observed travelers before they reached the house.

She witnessed departures as people returned to the road below.

For more than four decades, according to family tradition, Eliza remained associated with that place. The longevity of her presence suggests a degree of trust and continuity rarely acknowledged in formal records. A gatekeeper who remained in position for so many years would have become a familiar figure to neighbors and regular visitors alike.

The gate itself thus became part of her identity.

In the context of Monticello's history, such roles are often overshadowed by the prominence of the estate's owner. Yet examining the lives of individuals like Eliza Coleman allows historians to see the plantation from another perspective. The story shifts from the summit of the hill to the threshold below—from the famous house to the gate that controlled access to it.

Within that shift lies a broader historical insight.

Monticello was not simply a monument to political philosophy or architectural innovation. It was a lived environment where people worked, married, raised children, and built families under circumstances shaped by the realities of their time.

The lives of Eliza and Thomas Coleman illustrate how individuals navigated those realities while sustaining bonds of family and community.

Monticello was home to the Coleman and Henderson families for over a century, much longer than for anyone who held title to the property. Beginning in the 1860s, generations of these families greeted visitors at the Monticello gate and gave tours of the house and grounds. They worked first for the Levy family, Monticello's owners from 1879 to 1923, as cooks, gardeners, ox team drivers, and household employees.

Eliza Coleman was Monticello's gatekeeper during the Levy era. According to family tradition, she "came out of that Jefferson tree," but her connection to Monticello's enslaved families is not yet known. Her husband, Thomas Coleman, was the former slave of Joel Wheeler, who managed Monticello during and after the Civil War. Many Coleman descendants continue to live in Albemarle County. Eliza Coleman's great-great-grandson Paul Harris was elected to Thomas Jefferson's former seat in the House of Delegates in 1997 and again in 1999.

Getting Word

Their story is also part of a larger lineage.

The descendants of Eliza and Thomas carried forward memories of their ancestors' connection to Monticello. Those memories—sometimes preserved through documents, sometimes through oral tradition—became threads linking past generations to the present. Each recollection adds another layer to the understanding of how ordinary lives intersected with one of the most famous estates in American history.

Seen from the road, Monticello appears distant and elevated.

Seen from the gatehouse, it becomes part of the daily landscape of a family whose life unfolded at its entrance.

For Eliza Coleman, the gate was more than a workplace. It was the setting in which her marriage, her family, and her decades of service took place. The house above the hill remained a symbol of national history, but the gate below tells another story—one grounded in the lived experience of those who stood at the boundary between public legend and private life.

And it is from that boundary that the history of the Coleman family begins to emerge more clearly.

Courtesy Monticello

Mary Elizabeth Henderson, a distant relative of Harris, was the Monticello gatekeeper for almost 50 years.

Another Family Gatekeeper

Chapter Three — The Work of Watching

History often remembers great houses through the names of their owners. Yet the continuity of a place is often preserved by families whose lives remain rooted there across generations. At the entrance to Monticello, such continuity existed through the lives of three related women: Eliza Coleman, her daughter Lucy Coleman Barnaby Page, and their distant relative by marriage Mary Elizabeth Henderson.

Across successive generations, these women served as gatekeepers to the estate, each dedicating more than thirty years to the same responsibility. Their lives form a rare example of a family tradition connected to a single place for over a century.

Eliza Coleman

The story begins with Eliza Coleman, who lived and worked at Monticello during the lifetime of Thomas Jefferson. Family records and oral history describe Eliza as the gatekeeper at the entrance to the estate, where she lived near the gatehouse and managed the opening through which travelers entered the property.

During her years at Monticello, Eliza married Thomas Coleman Jr., a man whose father Thomas Coleman Sr. was believed to be a slave set free by Joel Wheeler. Together they established a household and raised children within the community that surrounded the plantation.

For more than forty years, Eliza stood watch at the gate, witnessing the steady movement of visitors, wagons, and travelers arriving from the surrounding countryside of Charlottesville.

Her long service created a foundation for what would become a remarkable family tradition.

A Legacy Passed from Mother to Daughter

When Eliza Coleman began her life at Monticello, the plantation existed within the deeply complex world of early American society.

The estate was owned by Thomas Jefferson, whose prominence in the founding of the United States has long overshadowed the many lives that unfolded within the boundaries of his Virginia plantation.

Eliza's responsibilities as gatekeeper placed her in a position of both duty and visibility. The gate marked the transition between public road and private estate.

Travelers approaching the mountain encountered the gate before they reached the house itself, and the person stationed there became the first human presence representing the property.

For more than forty years, according to family tradition, Eliza maintained that position.

Her life at the gatehouse was not merely a function of labor but also of residence and family. She had married Thomas Coleman Jr., and together they raised children while living within the orbit of Monticello.

Among those children was her daughter Lucy Coleman Barnaby Page, who grew up within sight of the very gate her mother watched over each day.

Children raised in such environments often inherited not only the physical spaces around them but also the responsibilities tied to those spaces. Lucy Coleman's life would follow a path that mirrored her mother's in an extraordinary way.

Lucy Coleman Barnaby Page and the Inherited Gate

As Lucy grew into adulthood, the landscape of Monticello itself was changing. The early nineteenth century brought economic uncertainty to the estate, and the death of Jefferson in 1826 altered the ownership and administration of the property. Despite these shifts, the physical structures of the mountain—the roads, buildings, and entrances—remained part of the lived environment of the people who continued to reside nearby.

Lucy Coleman Barnaby Page eventually assumed the role that had defined much of her mother's life.

Like Eliza before her, Lucy became the gatekeeper at Monticello. The position required constancy more than ceremony. Each day involved opening and closing the gate, observing those who approached the estate, and maintaining a presence at the boundary where travelers entered the property.

What makes Lucy's story particularly remarkable is the length of her service.

Family history holds that Lucy remained in the role for over thirty years, a span that echoes the decades her mother had spent at the same gate. The repetition of that number—forty years for Eliza, and more than thirty years again for Lucy—suggests not coincidence but continuity.

For two generations, the Coleman family maintained a steady presence at the entrance to Monticello.

Visitors arriving at the estate across those decades may not have realized they were witnessing the continuation of a family legacy. Yet for those who lived in the surrounding community of Charlottesville and throughout Albemarle County, such familiarity would have been unmistakable.

The gatehouse was not simply a structure; it was a place associated with the same family across generations.

Mary Elizabeth Henderson

The story did not end with Lucy.

Mary Elizabeth Henderson became a gatekeeper at Monticello during a later period in the estate's history, long after the era of Jefferson himself had passed into the realm of national memory.

By this time, Monticello had begun to evolve from a working plantation into a historic landmark that attracted increasing public attention. Visitors came not only as neighbors or business associates but also as travelers interested in the home of one of America's founding figures.

Even in that changing environment, the gate remained a place of human presence.

And like the women who had stood there before her, Mary Elizabeth Henderson served for over forty years.

Her decades at the gatehouse extended the tradition of long service that had begun with Eliza Coleman and continued through Lucy Coleman. Though separated by generations and historical circumstances, these women shared the same physical space and the same daily responsibility: standing at the boundary between the road and the estate.

A Tradition of Thirty Years or more

The number itself carries weight.

Thirty years represents more than employment; it signifies a lifetime of commitment to a place.

To serve at the gate for such a period means witnessing the passage of generations—watching children grow into adults, observing neighbors come and go, and seeing the surrounding landscape slowly change over time.

For Eliza Coleman, forty years meant guarding the entrance during the lifetime of Jefferson himself.

For Lucy Coleman, it meant continuing that watch through the decades that followed.

For Mary Elizabeth Henderson, it meant standing at the gate as Monticello transitioned into a site of historical

remembrance.

Across these different eras, the gatehouse remained a constant point in the geography of the mountain.

The View from the Gate

To stand at the gate of Monticello is to occupy a unique vantage point.

Looking upward, one sees the hill rising toward the famous house designed by Thomas Jefferson—a structure celebrated for its architecture and symbolism in American history.

Looking outward, one sees the road stretching toward the broader world of Virginia's countryside.

The gatekeeper stands between those two perspectives.

For the women who held that role across generations, the gate represented both responsibility and residence. It was a workplace, a home, and a place where history quietly unfolded in the daily routine of opening and closing the entrance to the estate.

Their stories rarely appear in official histories.

Yet the endurance of their presence tells its own story about the people whose lives formed the foundation of Monticello's everyday existence.

Remembering the Women of the Gate

In recovering the history of Eliza Coleman, Lucy Coleman, and Mary Elizabeth Henderson, we begin to see Monticello not only as a monument but also as a community shaped by the lives of those who lived and worked there.

These women were not architects of the famous house, nor were they political figures whose writings shaped a nation.

Their legacy lies elsewhere—in constancy, in presence, and in the quiet authority of watching over the entrance to a place that would become one of America's most visited historic sites.

For more than a century, the gate of Monticello was guarded by women whose service measured in decades.

Their lives remind us that history does not belong only to the house at the top of the hill.

Sometimes it belongs to the people who stood at the gate.

A Century at the Gate

When considered together, the lives of Eliza Coleman, Lucy Coleman, and Mary Elizabeth Henderson reveal a remarkable pattern of continuity.

Each woman lived within sight of the same road. Each opened and closed the same entrance. Each served for more than four decades.

Through them, the gate of Monticello was watched over by members of the same extended family for what may have been well over a century.

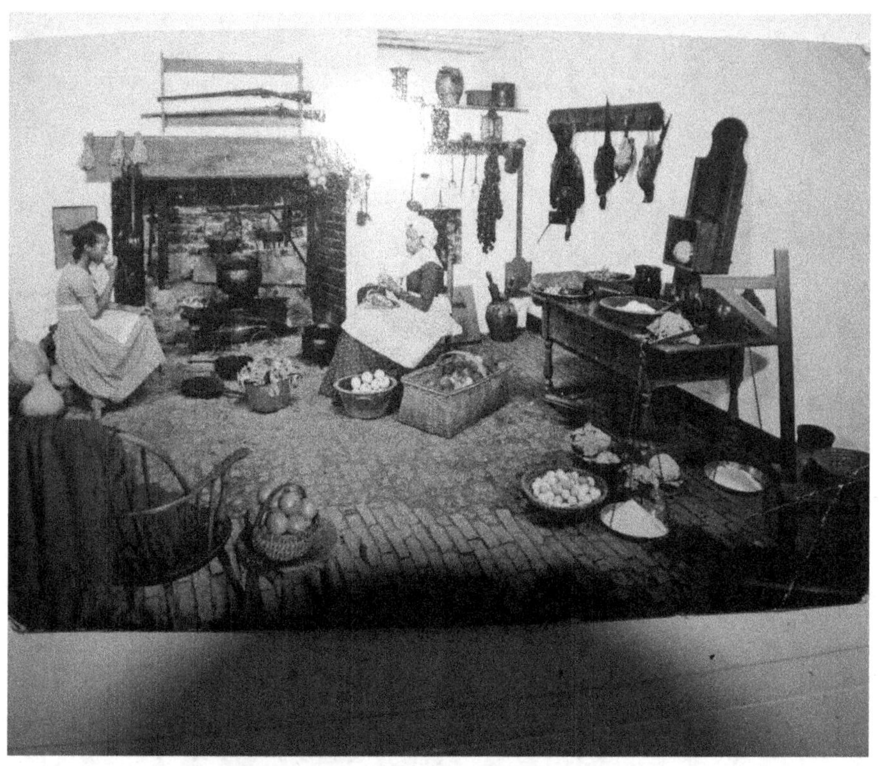

My Aunt Lucy Harris Briggs eating an apple at Monticello and my cousin Kate Jones. Rifles on the wall and wild game hanging up too

While the house on the hill has long been associated with the legacy of Thomas Jefferson, the gate below carries

another story—a story of women whose lives were defined by steadiness, responsibility, and presence.

Their legacy reminds us that history is not only shaped by those who lived in the grand house above, but also by those who stood faithfully at the entrance below.

The Gate with kids inside

Monticello, Main House

Chapter Four — The Road to the Mountaintop

The road that winds toward the summit of Monticello is both literal and symbolic. For visitors today, it is simply the

path that leads upward to the famous home of Thomas Jefferson. Yet for the descendants of the families who lived and labored in the world surrounding Monticello, that road represents something far deeper.

It is a road that connects generations, linking the lives of those who once stood at the gates of the estate to the descendants who now seek to understand their place within that history.

For me, that journey began far from Virginia.

My life began in the historic city of Trenton, a place with its own powerful place in American history. Trenton once served as the capital of the United States during the early years of the republic, and it was the site of one of the pivotal battles of the American Revolution. But long before I came to understand those national stories, Trenton was simply home.

It was in that city that I first heard the names of the people who came before me.

Like many children growing up in extended families, I learned about my ancestors gradually. Some names were spoken often and attached to vivid stories. Others appeared only occasionally in conversations among older relatives. Yet over time those names began to form a pattern—a lineage stretching back through generations to a place far beyond New Jersey.

That place was Charlottesville, Virginia.

The story begins with my great-great-grandmother, Eliza Tolliver
Coleman.

Eliza lived during a period when Virginia's social and economic
landscape was shaped by the plantation system.

Her life became closely associated with Monticello, the estate built
and occupied by Thomas Jefferson, third president of the United
States and author of the Declaration of Independence.

Family history records that Eliza served as a gatekeeper at
Monticello for more than forty years.

The gate she watched over was not merely a physical structure
marking the entrance to the estate. It was a point of transition
between two worlds: the public road traveled by visitors and
neighbors, and the private domain of the plantation itself. Those who
approached the mountain estate would encounter the gate before
reaching the house above.

In this way, Eliza Coleman stood at the threshold of one of the most
historically significant places in America.

Her life, however, was not defined solely by her responsibilities at the gate. She was also the matriarch of a large family. Eliza Tolliver Coleman had **eight children**, and through them the Coleman lineage spread outward across generations.

Among those children were two daughters whose lives would play important roles in the continuation of the family story.
One was Grace Coleman, my great-grandmother.

The other was Lucy Coleman Banaby Page, who would follow in her mother's footsteps as a gatekeeper at Monticello.

The story of Lucy Coleman Barnaby Page reflects the extraordinary continuity that sometimes occurs within families whose lives are tied to a particular place. Growing up near the entrance to the estate, Lucy would have witnessed the daily rhythms of her mother's responsibilities—opening and closing the gate, greeting visitors, and maintaining the boundary between the road and the property.

Eventually Lucy succeeded her mother as gatekeeper.

Like Eliza before her, Lucy served in that role for decades, continuing the family's association with the entrance to Monticello. Through mother and daughter, the Coleman family maintained a visible presence at the gateway to Jefferson's estate for a remarkable span of time.

While Lucy remained connected to Monticello, another branch of the family line emerged through the descendants of Grace Coleman.

Grace Coleman married Henry Harris, forming the union that joined the Coleman and Harris families. Their marriage produced a son who would become central to the next generation of the lineage.

That son was Joseph Henry Harris Sr., my grandfather. Joseph Henry Harris Sr. later married Rosa Smith Harris, and together they created a large and vibrant family whose descendants would extend the lineage across many branches.

Joseph and Rosa Harris had ten children, each representing a new stem in the expanding family tree.

**Their children included: Francine Harris,
Louise Harris Carr Fernandez, Grace Harris Brooks, Lucy
Harris Briggs, Sylvia Page Harris Coles, Estelle Harris Phox,
Pauline Harris Jackson, Margaret Harris Page, Joseph Harris
Jr.,
and Hugh L. Harris.**

Through these ten siblings, the Harris family expanded across
multiple communities and generations.

**Louise Harris Carr Fernandez raised a large family of her own.
Her children include Paulette Harris, Rose Marie,
Grace Robin, Esterlina, Sandra, Shirley, Sherry, and a son
named Sam.
Grace Harris Brooks had three children: Anthony Brooks,
Barbara Ann Loman, and Mildred Brooks.
Lucy Harris Briggs had a daughter named Jacqueline Hoefler.
Sylvia Page Harris Coles had four children: William Coles Jr.,
Rosana Coles, Abena Kerri Marysl, and Kelli
Coles.
Estelle Harris Phox had six children: Deborah, Johnny Harris,
Charles Phox, Lisa Phox Khan, Cynthia Phox Foy,
and Barry Phox.
Pauline Harris Jackson had three children: Roland Harris,
Sherry Young Jones, and Paul Clinton Harris, Esq.**

Paul Clinton Harris later served as a delegate representing Virginia's 58th District, a position that carries historical resonance. The district had once been represented by Thomas Jefferson, linking the political legacy of Jefferson to the descendant lineage of families who once lived within the world surrounding Monticello.

Margaret Harris Page had three children: Alfred Page, Donzell Page, and Aubrey Page.

Joseph Harris Jr. continued another branch of the Harris line.

My father, Hugh L. Harris, became another central figure in the family story.

He married my mother, Alice Carter Harris, joining the Harris family with the Carter family lineage.

Together they had two sons. My brother, Kevin Brian Harris. And myself, Hugh Lafon Carter.

My brother Kevin Brian Harris later had two sons of his own: Apostle Everton W. Harris Sr. and Kevin Michael

Harris, extending the family line into yet another generation.

Our family story also includes additional branches that connect through both parents.

My mother, Alice Carter Harris, had a daughter named Wetonah Carter, whose father was Gus Vincent, a man

believed to be related to former professional football player and NFL executive Troy Vincent.

My father, Hugh Lovejoy Harris, also had another son named Craig Hoagland with Bonnie Hoagland.

The Carter family itself includes several siblings of my mother: Earnest Johnson, David Carter, Jesse Carter,

James Carter, and Jerome Carter.

Through them, the Carter branch of the family spreads into additional generations and households.

Yet the story extends further still through the ancestry of my grandmother Rosa Smith Harris.

Rosa Smith Harris was the granddaughter of Charles Sampson Sr. and Laura Sampson, a couple whose large family formed another significant branch of the lineage.

**Charles and Laura Sampson had twelve children:Daisy
Sampson Smith, Rosa Sampson Peterson, Charles Sampson Jr.,
Cornelia Sampson Dredden, Robert Sampson, Jacob Sampson,
Selton Sampson,
Lena Sampson, Helen Sampson Smith, Hampton Sampson, Irene
Sampson,
and Frank Sampson.**

Among these children, Helen Sampson Smith became the mother of
Rosa Smith Harris.

Helen Sampson Smith raised a large family of her own. Her children
included James Henry Smith, Rosa Smith

Harris, Helen Smith Wesley, Edward Smith, Warren Smith, Hampton
Smith, Joseph Smith, Thomas W. Smith, and Bernard C. Smith.

Hampton Smith later had a daughter named Linda Smith Battle.

Other branches of the Sampson family also continued through later generations. Daisy Sampson Smith had a daughter named Lillie Calloway. Rosa Sampson Peterson had a daughter named Rosa. Charles Sampson Jr. had two daughters:

Daisy S. Moore and Carrie Juanita Sampson. Cornelia Sampson Dredden had a son named George Dredden Jr. Selton Sampson had a daughter named Marian Sampson Bland.

Several members of the Sampson family had no known children, including Robert Sampson, Jacob Sampson, Hampton Sampson, Irene Sampson, and Frank Sampson.

Taken together, these many names represent a vast web of relationships connecting multiple families across generations.

For many years these names existed primarily as memories shared within family conversations.

But in 1994, my personal connection to this history changed in a profound way.

That was the year I began traveling from Trenton, New Jersey to Charlottesville, Virginia.

The journey south brought me into the physical landscape where my ancestors had once lived. The road

that winds toward Monticello gradually climbs the mountain, offering a view of the surrounding countryside that has changed far less than many places in America.

Standing there, one begins to imagine what earlier generations may have seen.

The road approaching the gate.

The wagons and travelers arriving from distant communities.

The presence of the gatekeeper who stood at that entrance for decades.

President Thomas Jefferson

For me, the journey from Trenton to Charlottesville was more than a geographical trip.

It was the beginning of a deeper exploration into the history of my own family.

The road to the mountaintop had existed long before I was born.

But in 1994, I finally began to follow it.

And in doing so, I began to rediscover the generations whose lives had unfolded along that same path.

Thomas Jefferson (1743–1826) was an American Founding Father, the principal drafter of the Declaration of Independence, and the third President of the United States

(1801–1809). He is notable for shaping early U.S. institutions, promoting Enlightenment ideas about liberty and religious freedom, and for a lasting but deeply contested legacy because he was a large slaveholder.

Key facts
Born: April 13, 1743, Shadwell, Virginia. • Died: July 4, 1826, Monticello.
Major roles: Delegate, Secretary of State, Vice President, 3rd President.
•

Independence; architect of the Louisiana Purchase (1803). Signature acts: Author of the Declaration of
86
• Other: Founded the University of Virginia; lifelong owner of enslaved people.

Early life and political rise

Raised on a Virginia plantation, Jefferson trained as a lawyer and entered the Virginia legislature, where he advanced reforms including the Virginia Statute for Religious Freedom. He emerged nationally as the principal author of the Declaration of Independence in 1776 and later served in diplomatic and cabinet posts before becoming president.

Presidency and public projects

As president he completed the Louisiana Purchase, doubling U.S. territory, and promoted agrarian republicanism and public education. He designed architectural projects (notably Monticello) and later founded the University of Virginia to advance secular higher education.

Legacy and controversies

Jefferson's writings advanced rights and separation of church and state, yet his life embodied contradictions: he authored "all men are created equal" while owning hundreds of enslaved people and expressing racist views in works like Notes on the State of Virginia. Modern scholarship and public debate continue to reassess his achievements alongside the harms of slavery tied to his wealth and household.

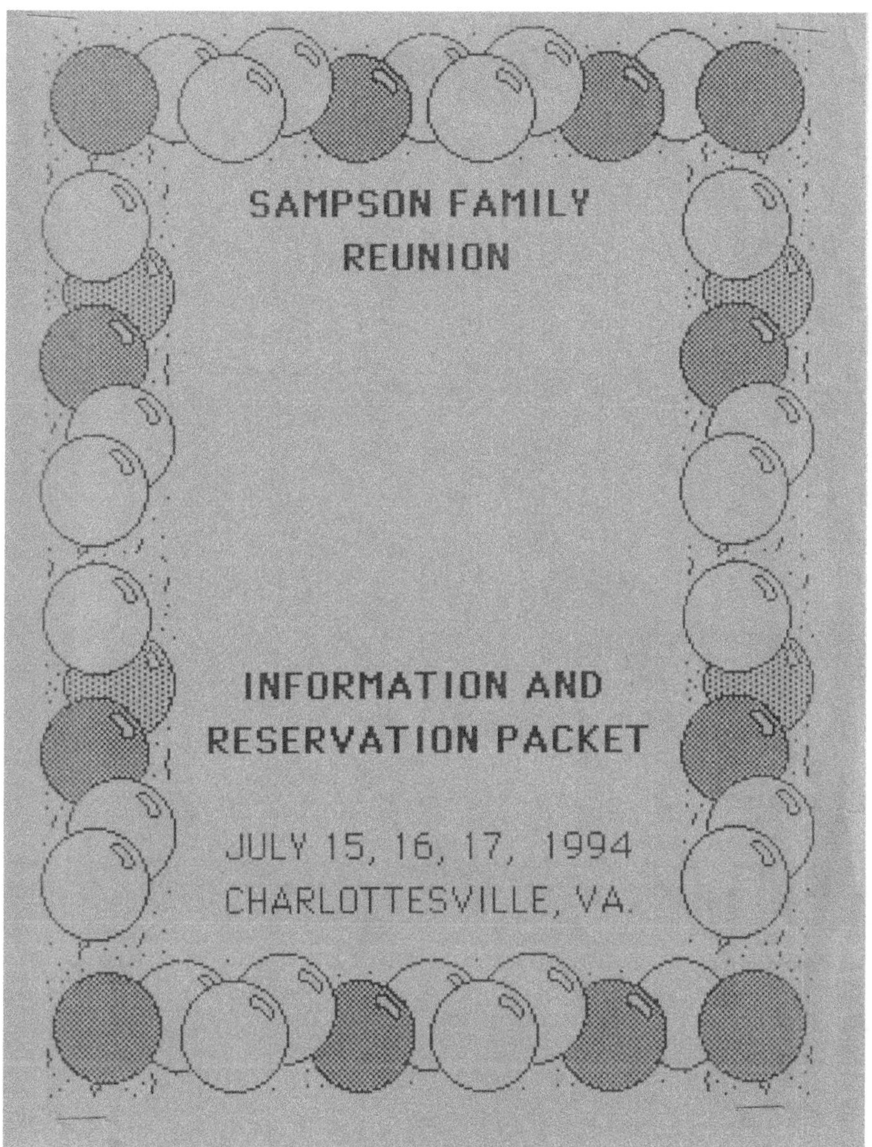

My First Sampson Family Reunion

Program 1994

**Monticello Declaration of Independence University of Virginia
Sally Hemings
Monticello**

Monticello is the historic estate designed and built by Thomas Jefferson, located near Charlottesville, Virginia. Recognized as a masterpiece of neoclassical architecture

and a symbol of the early American republic, it reflects Jefferson's intellectual curiosity and his vision for a self- sufficient agrarian life. The property is both a UNESCO World Heritage Site and a U.S. National Historic Landmark.

Key facts

**Location: Charlottesville, Virginia, USA Architect: Thomas Jefferson Construction period: 1768–1809 Designation: UNESCO World Heritage Site
(1987)
Managed by: Thomas Jefferson Foundation**

Architecture and Design

Monticello embodies Jefferson's synthesis of Enlightenment ideals and classical design.

Inspired by Italian Renaissance architect Andrea Palladio, Jefferson created a residence that balanced symmetry and function. Its red-brick façade, columned portico, and octagonal dome were pioneering features in 18th-century America. The house also integrated Jefferson's innovations, including hidden dumbwaiters, alcove beds, and advanced ventilation systems.

Plantation and Daily Life

The 5,000-acre plantation was both Jefferson's home and a working agricultural enterprise dependent on the labor of enslaved African Americans. Enslaved workers

cultivated crops, produced goods, and maintained the estate.

Modern interpretation at Monticello emphasizes their lives and contributions, notably those of the Hemings

family, whose history is intertwined with Jefferson's own.

Legacy and Interpretation

Today, Monticello serves as a museum and educational center dedicated to Jefferson's complex legacy—his authorship of the Declaration of Independence and his ownership of enslaved people.

The Thomas Jefferson Foundation offers guided tours, digital archives, and public programs that explore Enlightenment thought, early American democracy, and the contradictions of liberty and slavery.

Cultural Impact

Monticello remains a powerful symbol of the American experiment in self-governance and architecture. Its image

appears on the U.S. nickel and in numerous cultural references, representing both the ideals and contradictions of the nation's founding era.

Eliza Coleman at the gate of Monticello in 1912

Chapter Five — After Jefferson: Monticello In Transition

When Thomas Jefferson died on July 4, 1826, the future of Monticello entered a period of uncertainty and transition.

The estate that Jefferson had designed and cultivated over decades was no longer guided by its creator. Financial difficulties and the complexities of settling Jefferson's debts meant that Monticello could not remain unchanged.

For the many individuals whose lives were connected to the mountain—including laborers, craftsmen, and families who lived in the surrounding community—the years following Jefferson's death marked the beginning of a new era.

Monticello had always been more than a residence. It was the center of a large agricultural enterprise and a community shaped by the plantation system of early Virginia. The estate included fields, workshops, quarters, and roads that connected it to nearby settlements throughout Charlottesville and Albemarle County.

When Jefferson died, the plantation economy that supported Monticello was already weakening. The estate's finances were strained, and Jefferson's heirs faced the difficult task of resolving substantial debts.

As a result, Monticello itself was sold.

In 1831 the property passed out of Jefferson family ownership when it was purchased by a local pharmacist named James Turner Barclay. Barclay's ownership marked the first major transition in the history of the estate after Jefferson's lifetime.

Yet the physical landscape of the mountain did not immediately change.

The road still wound upward toward the summit. The gates still marked the boundaries of the property. And the surrounding countryside remained familiar to the families who had lived and worked there for generations.

Among those families were the descendants of Eliza Tolliver Coleman.

Eliza Coleman had served as a gatekeeper during the Jefferson era. Her long tenure at the entrance to Monticello had placed her at a unique intersection between the estate and the wider world beyond its boundaries.

After her years of service, the responsibility of guarding the gate
passed to her daughter Lucy Coleman Barnaby Page.

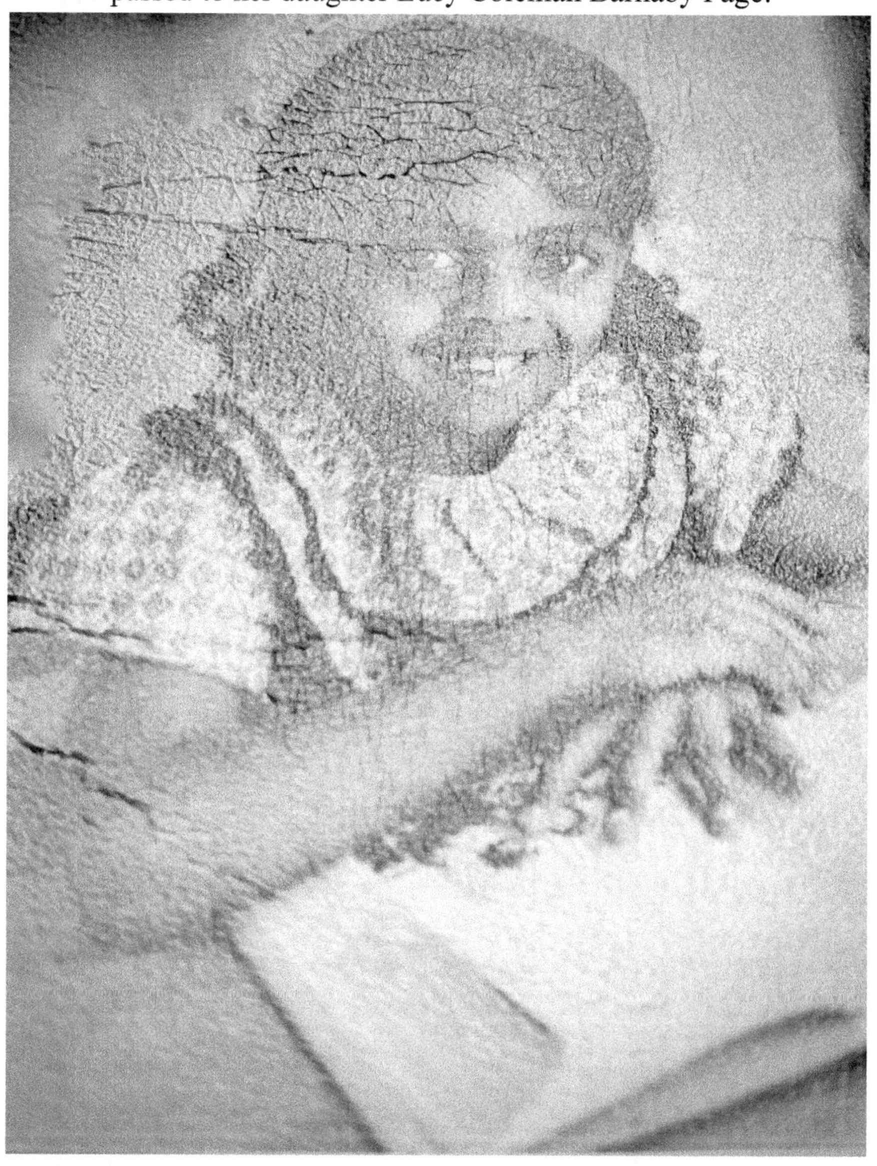

My mother Alice Harris in school 1940's.Thank you!

Lucy continued the tradition established by her mother. For decades she remained associated with the gate at Monticello, greeting travelers and observing the steady flow of people who arrived along the mountain road.

The period following Jefferson's death therefore did not erase the presence of families like the Colemans. Instead, their lives continued to shape the everyday experience of the estate even as ownership changed.

After Barclay's brief ownership, Monticello changed hands again.

In 1834 the estate was purchased by Uriah P. Levy, a naval officer and prominent advocate of Jefferson's legacy.

Levy admired Jefferson deeply and believed the house should be preserved as a national monument honoring the author of the Declaration of Independence.

Levy's acquisition of Monticello marked an important turning point in the preservation of the property.

Although the estate remained privately owned, Levy devoted considerable effort and personal resources to restoring Jefferson's home, which had fallen into disrepair during the years following Jefferson's death.

During this period the landscape of Monticello continued to evolve.

The plantation economy that had once defined the estate gradually faded, and the mountain increasingly became known as a place of historical significance rather than agricultural production. Visitors began arriving not only for business or travel but also out of curiosity about Jefferson's home.

Throughout these changes, the gate remained an essential point of arrival.

It was here that the legacy of the Coleman family continued through generations of gatekeepers.

After Lucy Coleman Barnaby Page, the responsibility of guarding the entrance eventually passed to Try Elizabeth Henderson, a distant relative within the extended family network.

Henderson's years of service extended the tradition of long stewardship at the gate. Like Eliza and Lucy before her, she remained associated with the entrance to Monticello for decades.

Through these women the gate of Monticello became more than an architectural feature. It became a place of continuity.

Across successive generations, members of the same extended family watched over the road leading to the mountain.

Meanwhile, Monticello itself was entering a new phase of its history.

In the late nineteenth century the estate eventually came under the stewardship of the Thomas Jefferson

Foundation, which transformed the property into a museum dedicated to preserving Jefferson's home and interpreting the complex history of the plantation.

Today visitors from around the world travel to Monticello to learn about Jefferson's life and the broader history of early America.

Yet beyond the famous architecture and political legacy lies another story—the story of the families whose lives unfolded in the shadow of the mountain.

Among those families were the descendants of Eliza Coleman.

Their connection to the gate at Monticello reminds us that the history of the estate is not only the story of a president and philosopher. It is also the story of the people who lived and worked along the road that leads to the mountaintop.

The Coleman Gatekeepers of Monticello
18th Century
c. Late 1700s
Eliza Tolliver Coleman begins living and working at Monticello during the lifetime of Thomas Jefferson. c. 1780s–1820s
Eliza Coleman serves as gatekeeper at the entrance to Monticeelo, reportedly for more than forty years.
Early 19th Century
1826
Death of Thomas Jefferson.
1826–1830s
Eliza Coleman's daughter Lucy Coleman Barnaby Page succeeds her mother as gatekeeper.
Mid-19th Century
1831
Monticello sold to James Turner Barclay.
1834
Monticello purchased by Uriah P. Levy, who begins restoring the estate.
Late 19th Century
Mid–late 1800s
Lucy Coleman Barnaby Page continues long service as gatekeeper.
Later period
Gatekeeping responsibility passes to Mary Elizabeth Henderson, a distant relative of the Coleman family.
Early Preservation Era Late 1800s–Early 1900s

Monticello becomes recognized as an important historic site.

Family

Chapter Six — The Descendants Return to the Mountain

History is not only preserved in archives, monuments, or museums.

It is also preserved in memory.

For generations, the story of the Coleman, Harris, Smith, Sampson, and Carter families lived primarily through spoken tradition. Elders remembered the names of ancestors, the locations of family land, and the connections that tied their lineage to the mountain estate known as Monticello.

But by the late twentieth century, those stories faced a challenge familiar to many families whose roots reach deep into American history: the passage of time.

As generations passed and relatives scattered across different states, pieces of the family narrative risked being lost.

It was within that context that a new chapter in the story began. The year was 1994.

At that time I was living in Trenton, the historic city where my own life had begun. Though I had long heard fragments of family history, I had not yet fully explored the deeper connections that tied my lineage to Virginia.

That changed when I traveled south to attend my first Sampson family reunion near Charlottesville.

For many families, reunions are simply opportunities to reconnect with relatives. For me, this gathering became something much more significant.

It became the moment when the past opened before me. When I arrived, I was welcomed by members of my father's family— particularly my father's sisters, my aunts— who greeted me warmly and introduced me to relatives I had never met before. Their embrace carried with it a sense of belonging that bridged years of distance.

They welcomed me not only as a nephew or cousin but as a member of a larger historical family. Among the relatives present were members of the Sampson family reunion committee, individuals who had taken on the responsibility of preserving and organizing the family's history.

These committee members had spent years gathering documents, recording stories, and tracing the lineage of the Sampson family back through generations.

During the reunion, they presented me with a remarkable gift.

They gave me a package containing family history materials—documents, genealogical notes, and records that had been carefully preserved and assembled.

Holding those papers in my hands, I realized that the history of my family was far richer and deeper than I had previously understood.

Those documents contained the names of ancestors, records of marriages and births, and references to places that had once been central to the lives of earlier generations.

But the most powerful moment came during a conversation among family members. At some point during the reunion, the topic of preserving the family's story arose. Several relatives expressed the belief that someone in the family should write a book documenting the history of the Sampson lineage and its connections to the surrounding community.

Anne Slaughter and four other descendants of Monticello gatekeeper Eliza Tolliver Coleman were interviewed together in 1995. All live in the Washington, DC, area and work (or worked) in various departments of the federal government. They shared their memories of Eliza Coleman's daughters Lucy Coleman Barnaby Page and Grace Coleman Harris and recalled summers spent at the Monticello gatehouse. Members of the extended Coleman family lived at Monticello for more than a century—far longer than any of the property's owners.

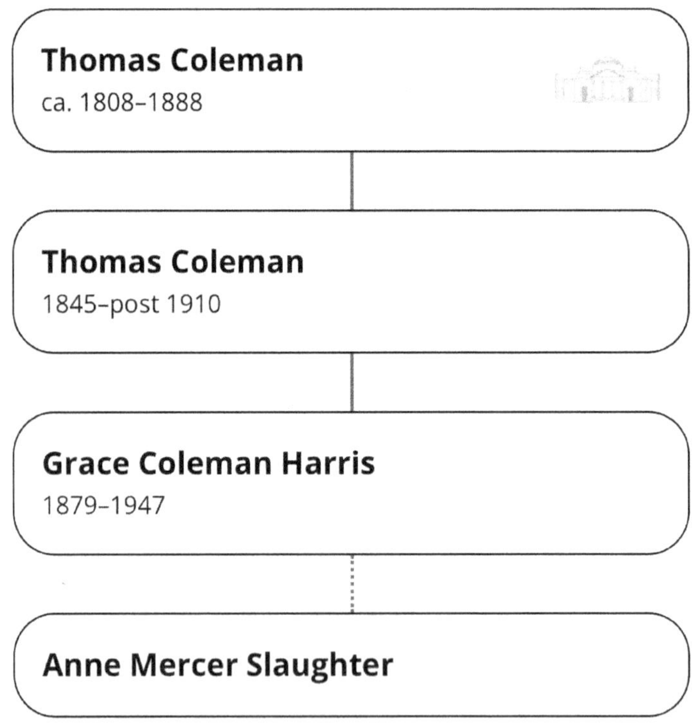

Anne Mercer Slaughter

Anne Slaughter and four other descendants of Monticello gatekeeper Eliza Tolliver Coleman were interviewed together in 1995. All live in the Washington, DC, area and work (or worked) in various departments of the federal government. They shared their memories of Eliza Coleman's daughters Lucy Coleman Barnaby Page and Grace Coleman Harris and recalled summers spent at the Monticello gatehouse. Members of the extended Coleman family lived at Monticello for more than a century—far longer than any of the property's owners.

They understood that oral history alone could not guarantee the survival of the story. Someone would

eventually have to write it down.

In that moment I made a promise.

I told them that one day I would write the book.

At the time, I did not yet know how long that journey would take, or how many discoveries would lie ahead. But

the seed had been planted.

The reunion did more than introduce me to family records.

It also introduced me to a place that held deep significance in the family's history.

Just a few miles south of Monticello, in the rural community of Simeon, members of the Sampson family

had once owned land that they called Rose Hill.

The land at Rose Hill represented something profoundly meaningful for descendants of families whose

ancestors had lived through slavery.

It represented ownership.

Generations earlier, the Sampson family had acquired property in Simeon and built homes there. They did more than establish residences. They created a community.

At the center of that community stood a Baptist church built by members of the family themselves.

The church served as more than a place of worship.

It was a gathering place, a school of moral instruction, and a symbol of collective identity. Within its walls, families celebrated weddings, mourned losses, and taught their children the values that would guide them through life.

Standing on that land in 1994, I realized that the story of my family extended far beyond individual ancestors.

It included entire communities built through determination, resilience, and faith.

The discovery of Rose Hill connected the past to the present in a tangible way.

Only a few miles separated the family land in Simeon from the mountain where Eliza Coleman had once served as gatekeeper at Monticello. Yet the historical distance between those places represented generations of struggle and progress.

From the gates of a plantation to land ownership and community building.

From servitude to self-determination.

The land known as Rose Hill represented more than a place on a map. For the Sampson family, it stood as a symbol of perseverance and independence.

Located near Simeon, just a few miles south of Monticello, Rose Hill became a place where members of the Sampson family established homes, raised children, and built a lasting community.

At the center of that community stood a Baptist church constructed by members of the family themselves. The

church served not only as a place of worship but also as a gathering place where generations came together for baptisms, weddings, funerals, and family celebrations.

What makes the story of Rose Hill especially meaningful is that the connection to that land did not end with earlier generations.

To this day, descendants of the Sampson family— including members of my own extended family—still retain ownership of portions of that land.

In a nation where many families lost ancestral property through time, migration, or economic hardship, the continued presence of Sampson descendants on land once established by their forebears stands as a rare and powerful testament to endurance.

It represents continuity.

It represents legacy.

And it represents the determination of a family to preserve its roots across generations.

Standing on that land in 1994, I understood something that had not been fully clear to me before.

The road to Monticello was not only a path leading upward to a historic house on a mountain.

It was also a road that led outward—to communities like Simeon and to family land like Rose Hill, where descendants transformed history into ownership, faith, and community.

In that moment, the story of my ancestors felt less like distant history and more like a living inheritance.

The book also tells the story of Rose Hill, family land near Simeon that remains partially owned by Sampson descendants to this day—a rare example of ancestral land preserved across generations.

The Sampson family reunion of 1994 therefore marked more than a social gathering.

It marked the beginning of a personal journey into historical research.

In the years that followed, I continued exploring the records and stories that had been shared with me that day.

Each document revealed new connections between family members and historical events.

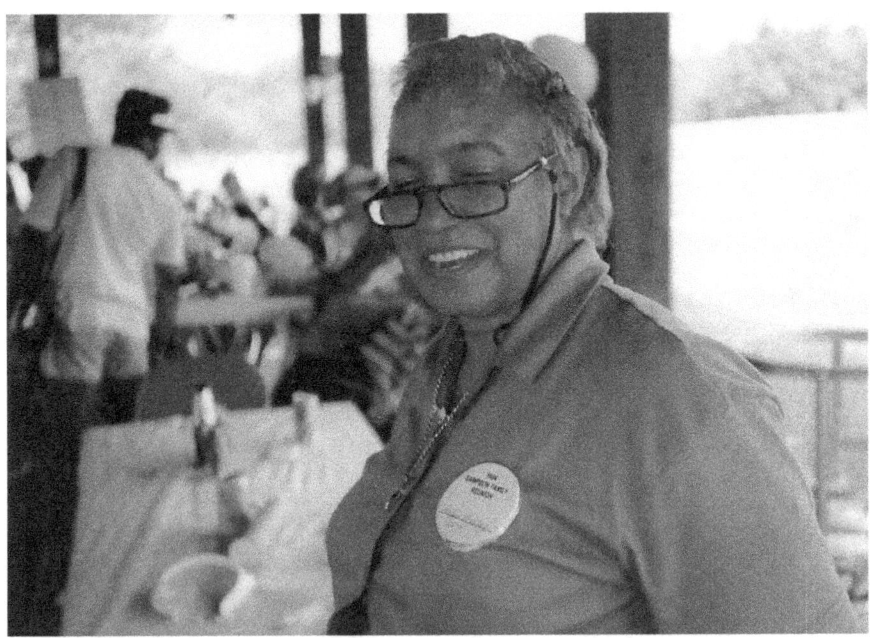

My great aunt Helen Wesley Smith 1994

Each name became a thread within a much larger tapestry.

The more I learned, the more I understood that the story of the Coleman, Sampson, and Harris families was not simply a private family history.It was part of the broader story of America.

It was the story of people whose lives intersected with one of the most famous historical sites in the nation.

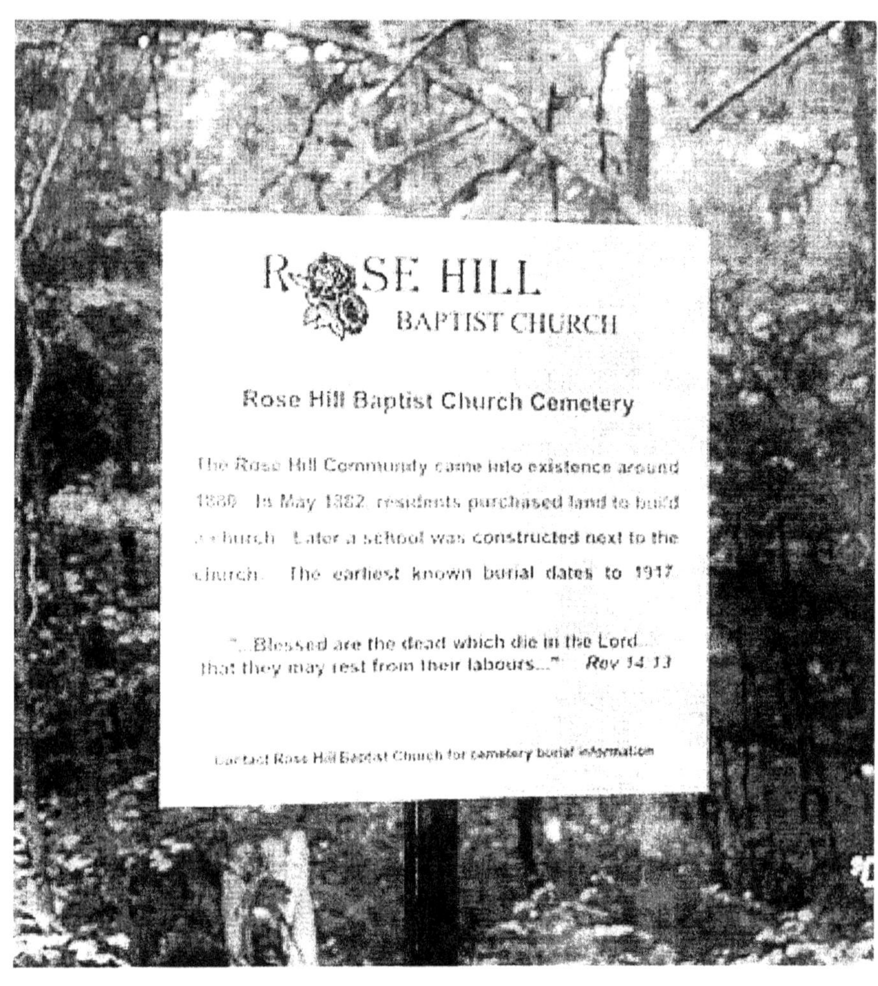

Rose Hill Community purchased in 1882

It was the story of descendants returning to the mountain.

My aunt Pauline, Sylvia, Grace, Lucy and Margaret

And it was the fulfillment of the promise I made that day in 1994.

A promise to write the story so that future generations would know where they came from.

Family Records and Historical Documents
Sampson Family Reunion Program (1994)

Program from the Sampson family reunion held in Charlottesville, Virginia, where descendants gathered to

celebrate their shared heritage and preserve family history.

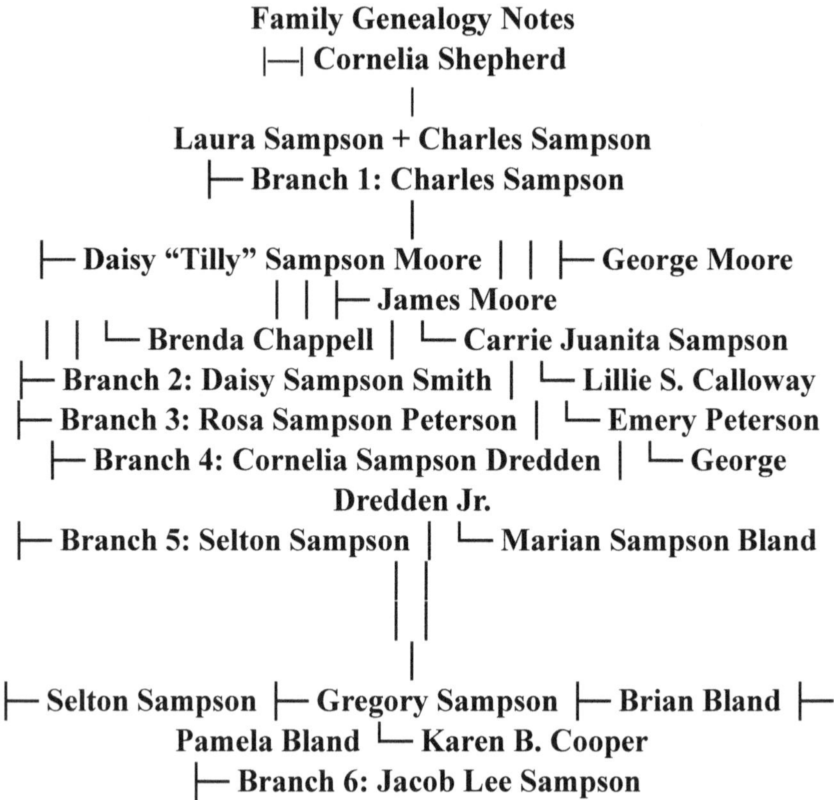

Family Genealogy Notes
|—| Cornelia Shepherd
Laura Sampson + Charles Sampson
├— Branch 1: Charles Sampson
├— Daisy "Tilly" Sampson Moore | | ├— George Moore
| | ├— James Moore
| | └— Brenda Chappell | └— Carrie Juanita Sampson
├— Branch 2: Daisy Sampson Smith | └— Lillie S. Calloway
├— Branch 3: Rosa Sampson Peterson | └— Emery Peterson
├— Branch 4: Cornelia Sampson Dredden | └— George Dredden Jr.
├— Branch 5: Selton Sampson | └— Marian Sampson Bland
├— Selton Sampson ├— Gregory Sampson ├— Brian Bland ├—
Pamela Bland └— Karen B. Cooper
├— Branch 6: Jacob Lee Sampson

├─ **Branch 7: Robert Sampson**
├─ **Branch 8: Helen Sampson Smith**
│   │ ├─ **Edward Smith**

•

│   │ ├─ **Warren Smith**
│ ├─ **Hampton Smith→ Linda S. Battle**
├─ **James "Bobby" Henry Smith → Travis Ross & April Burton**

│ ├─ **Joseph Smith** ├─ **Thomas W. Smith**
     ├─ **Bernard C. Smith**
     ├─ **Helen Smith Wesley**

├─ **Grace Harris Brooks → Barbara Loman & Tyheich Brooks**
├─ **Hugh Lovejoy Harris → Hugh Carter & Kevin Michael Harris**
  │ ├─ **Frances Harris** ├─ **Joseph H. Harris Jr.**
  └─ **Rosa Smith Harris** │ ├─ **Grace Harris**

├─ **Estelle Harris Phox → Charles Phox & Barry Phox**

│ ├─ **Sylvia Harris Coles**
├─ **Lucy Harris Briggs → Jaqueline Hoefler**
  └─ **Pauline Harris → Paul Clinton Harris**
     ├─ **Branch 9: Hampton Sampson**
├─ **Branch 10: Irene Sampson** ├─ **Branch 11: Lena Sampson**
     └─ **Branch 12: Frank Sampson**

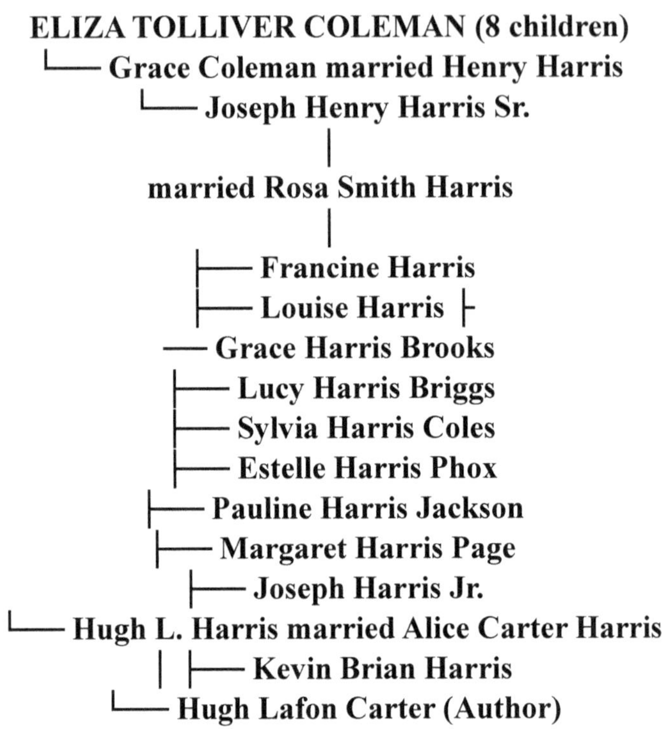

Genealogical research compiled by members of the Sampson family reunion committee.

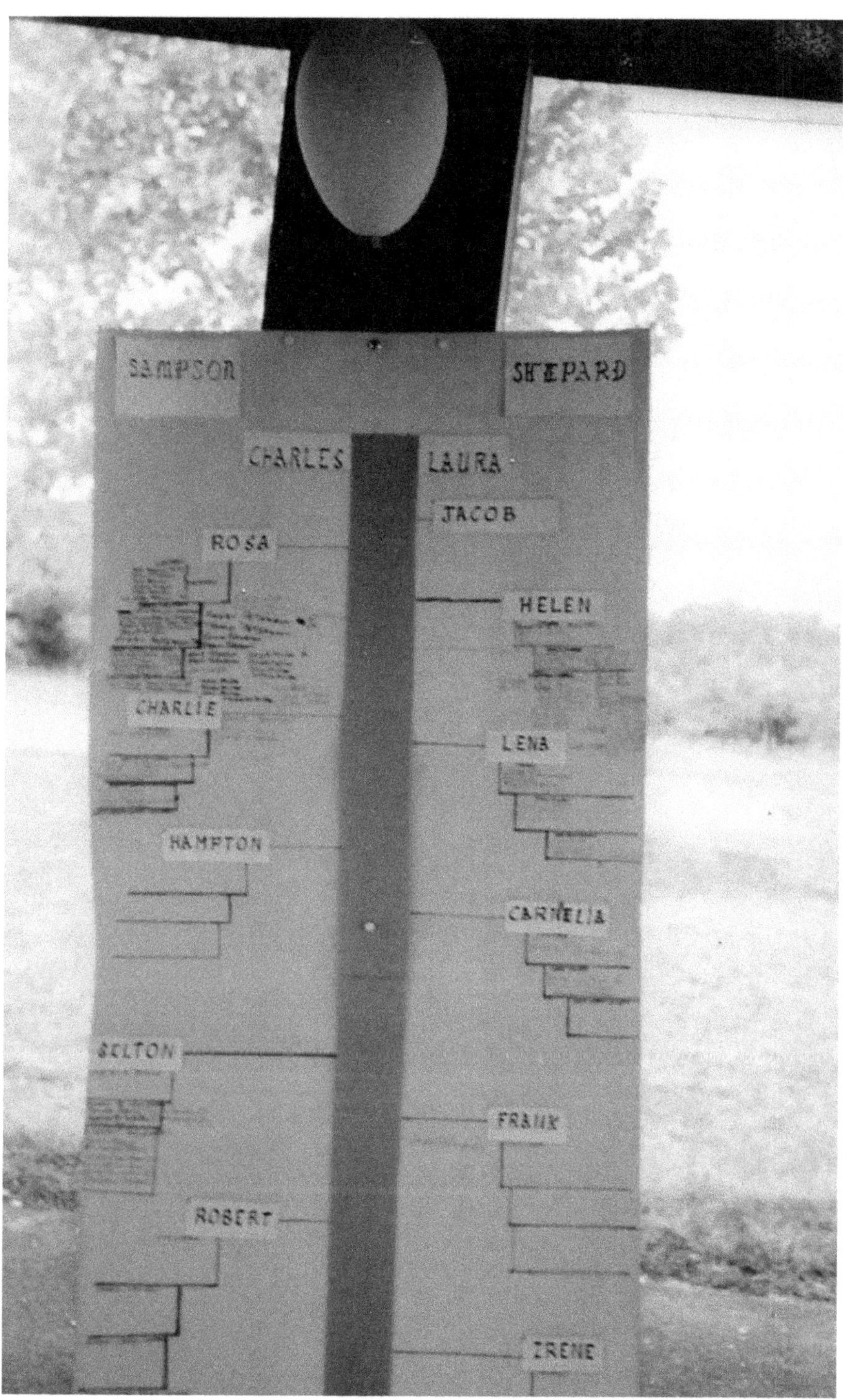

SAMPSON
SHEPARD
CHARLES
LAURA
JACOB
ROSA
HELEN
CHARLIE
LENA
HAMPTON
CARMELIA
BOLTON
FRANK
ROBERT
IRENE

THE SAMPSON FAMILY
5th
REUNION

Comfort Inn, Monticello
Charlottesville, Virginia

June 23, and June 24, 2007

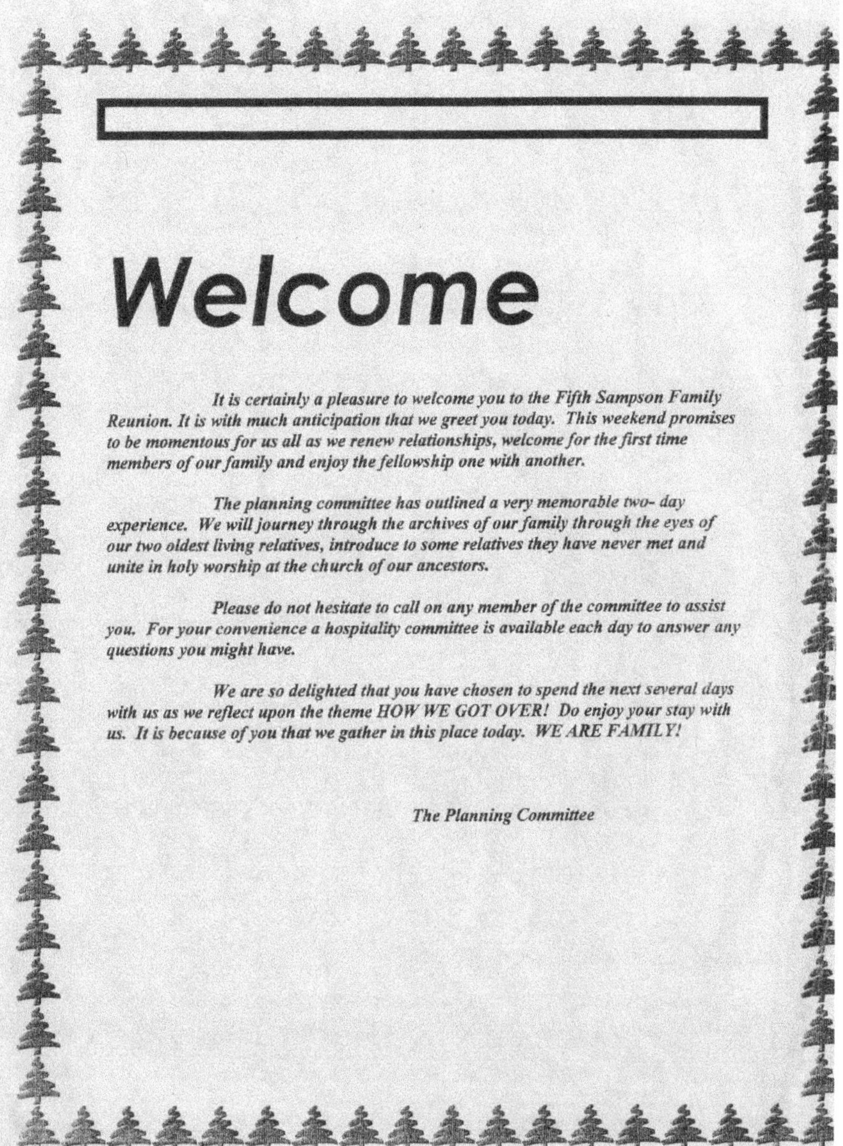

Welcome

It is certainly a pleasure to welcome you to the Fifth Sampson Family Reunion. It is with much anticipation that we greet you today. This weekend promises to be momentous for us all as we renew relationships, welcome for the first time members of our family and enjoy the fellowship one with another.

The planning committee has outlined a very memorable two- day experience. We will journey through the archives of our family through the eyes of our two oldest living relatives, introduce to some relatives they have never met and unite in holy worship at the church of our ancestors.

Please do not hesitate to call on any member of the committee to assist you. For your convenience a hospitality committee is available each day to answer any questions you might have.

We are so delighted that you have chosen to spend the next several days with us as we reflect upon the theme HOW WE GOT OVER! Do enjoy your stay with us. It is because of you that we gather in this place today. WE ARE FAMILY!

The Planning Committee

RALLY

In Honor of Founders

of the

ROSE HILL

BAPTIST CHURCH

∽

Sundry, November 16, 1958

7:30 P. M.

Program

∽

Devotions ....Led by Deacon Frank Sampson
and Deacon Bernard Smith

Welcome Address ....Mrs. Ellen Winston

Response ....Mrs. Elizabeth Mayo

Solo ....Mrs. Lelia Anderson

Sermon ....Rev. S. H. Miller

Music ....Shiloh Choir

Collection ....Deacon Mansfield Gunnell, Sr.
and Deacon Tanner

Remarks ....Deacon J. J. Truehart

Remarks ....Mr. George Hardy

Each one is asked to give a donation in
honor of your loved ones.

PROGRAM SUBMITTED

BY

Ann Slaughter Daughter of:

Martha 'Harris' Mercer

Granddaughter of:

Henry Harris

and

Gracie 'Coleman' Harris

The Founders of this Church

Rev. George Hardy, Sr., the pastor of the Mt. Zion Baptist Church, Charlottesville, .Virginia, preached the first sermon at this church in 1892.

The first founders of this church are as follows:

Deacon—Hillary Barnaby
Deacon—Micajah Henderson
Deacon—Toney Luck
Deacon—Daniel Carter

Some of the members that joined later:

Deacon—Enfield Grady
Deacon—Charles Sampson
Deacon—Richard Sampson
Deacon—Norris Carr
Deacon—Norman Smith
Deacon—Granville Dickerson
Deacon—Henry Harris, Sr.

Others later joined this church that we fail to name.

MRS. M. W. MITCHELL, M. C.
REV. J. H. ROBERTS, Pastor
MISS E. E. WINSTON, Clerk

Rose Hill Baptist Church 1958

Historical Land References – Rose Hill

But God commanded His love toward us in that while we were yet sinners, Christ died for us.   Romans 5:8

2421 Rose Hill Church Lane
Charlottesville, VA 22902
(434) 295-6441

PASTOR JEFFERY O. KING
(434) 985-3755 (HOME)
(434) 295-6441 (CHURCH)

SUNDAY, SUNDAY SCHOOL	9:30 A.M.
SUNDAY, PRAISE SERVICE	11:00 A.M.
SUNDAY, MORNINIG WORSHIP	11:30 A.M.
WEDNESDAY, BIBLE STUDAY	7:30 P.M.
FRIDAY, AWANA YOUTH MINISTRY	7:30 P.M.

(CONCURRENT WITH SCHOOL YEAR)

Come experience the fragrance of THE ROSE *where Jesus has risen in our hearts.*

Rose Hill Baptist Church Schedule

Sampson Family Fifth Family Reunion

Comfort Inn-Monticello
Charlottesville, Virginia
Saturday, June 23, 2007
One O'clock in the afternoon

P R O G R A M M E

Greetings/The Occasion   George M. Moore

The Invocation   Pastor Jeffery O. King
Senior Minister, Rose Hill Baptist Church

HOW   WE   GOT   OVER!

Who are we?   The Generations Speak

Lunch is Served

Beef vegetable soup
Tossed salad w/assorted dressings
Fried chicken
Ham steaks
Macaroni & cheese
Green beans
Buttered broccoli
Rolls w/butter
Carrot Cake   Chocolate Cake
Tea/Coffee/Water

A   Look into the Past

In Memorial   The Candle Lighting Ceremony
A view from the Past   Video Presentation

The Presentation of the Family Tree

Sampson Family Reunion Lunch

Rose Hill Baptist Church

Worship Service

1 Corinthians 10:31
Whether therefore ye eat, or drink, or whatsoever you do, do all to the glory of God.

MORNING DEVOTION
DECON OTTO BATES

CALL TO WORSHIP
PASTOR JEFFERY KING

OPENING HYMN
SENIOR ADULT CHOIR

INVOCATION
PASTOR JEFFERY KING

CHANT
SENIOR ADULT CHOIR
SHARE WITH YOUR NEIGHBORS
SCRIPTURE/PRAYER
TBA

WELCOME
TBA

ANNOUNCEMENTS
SISTER ANNETTE HENDERSON

MISSIONARY/TITHES/OFFERING
Deacons/Trustee(s)

Doxology (pg. 527)
Congregation

INSPIRATIONAL HYMN
SENIOR ADULT CHOIR

THE PREACHED WORD
PASTOR JEFFERY KING

INVITATION TO DISCIPLESHIP/BENEDICTION
PASTOR JEFFERY KING
(reprinted from Sunday, April 15, 2007)

Worship Service

Family Descendants

Family at Rosehill Baptist Church

The Original Church Constructed in 1891

Church letting out. 2005

ROSE HILL BAPTIST CHURCH
Simeon, Virginia

NEW CHURCH BUILD IN 1976

Albemarle Training School

We, the class of 1948 the first class to publish an Annual in the history of the school, now declare our creed.

First we believe in the Christian God who has led us to victory and granted us sucess.

Second, we believe that someday our potentilities shall blossom forth abundantly in deeds of good will for all people.

Third, we believe in our principal Mrs. Mary Carr Greer who has expressed her untiring interest and friendship for us in countless days.

Fourth, we believe in our teachers who with love, skill have sought to help us develop into worthy citizens.

Fifth, we beleive in our theme "Citizenship Through Education".

Sixth, we believe the portion of education we have obtained during our four years at Albemarle Training School will influence us to bend every effort to hasten the acquisition of that wisdom without which knowledge might be as dangerous as the Atom Bomb.

Seventh, but by no means least, we believe in our parents, whose uncomplaining sacrifices and endless patience have made our present development, possible, and whose prayers, and work have been for us in the past, and will be for us through eternity.

With this creed we go forth to build a better world.

ALMA MATER

In a rose tinted valley encircled by hills,

   Resting deep in a land that is blest,

Where the robins make merry their songs all the day,

   Lies the school that we love the best.

We will always adore Thee wherever we roam,

   Though our feet from Thy walls may depart,

As we mumur farewell to the days that are gone,

   And the mem'ry of one that is dear.

Though ages may come and we'll pass from these scenes

   While others our places may fill,

But we'll reverence Thy name dear old Albemarle School,

   And to Thee we will ever be true.

We will uphold Thy laws, both at school and abroad,

   As to hy standards we'll ever cling,

As we follow our motto: "Character and Courage.

   Perseverance" unto the end.

1948 Class Creed at The Albemarle Training School

Albemarle Training Center I took this image in 2007 of my Aunt and cousins. R.I.P.

Two miles south of Monticello, in the rural community of Simeon, Virginia, generations of families connected to the Coleman, Harris, Smith, and Sampson lines established homes, farms, and churches after the end of slavery. One of the most important institutions built by the community was Rose Hill Baptist Church, which served as both a spiritual center and a gathering place for the families who lived on and around Rose Hill.

Education also became a cornerstone of the community. Students from Rose Hill and surrounding areas attended Albemarle Training School, which served local children for many decades.

Although schools in Virginia during much of the early twentieth century operated under segregation laws, the daily life of rural communities was often more complex than the legal structure suggested.

Families of different backgrounds worked together in agriculture, trades, and local institutions connected to the school.

White residents, relatives and Black, residents, relatives alike were part of the broader community that supported the school and its activities, and the institution served as an important educational and vocational center for the region.

For the descendants of Eliza Tolliver Coleman, the history of Rose Hill and Albemarle Training School reflects the determination of families who valued learning and community. The school helped educate generations of local children and stood as a reminder that education was central to the future of the community.

57
AQI 40
RICHMOND RD
250
Monticello
Calle Branch
Indian Branch
MILTON RD
732
8 min
Fastest
2421 Rose Hill
Church Ln
Henderso
JEFFER
MILTON RD
N M

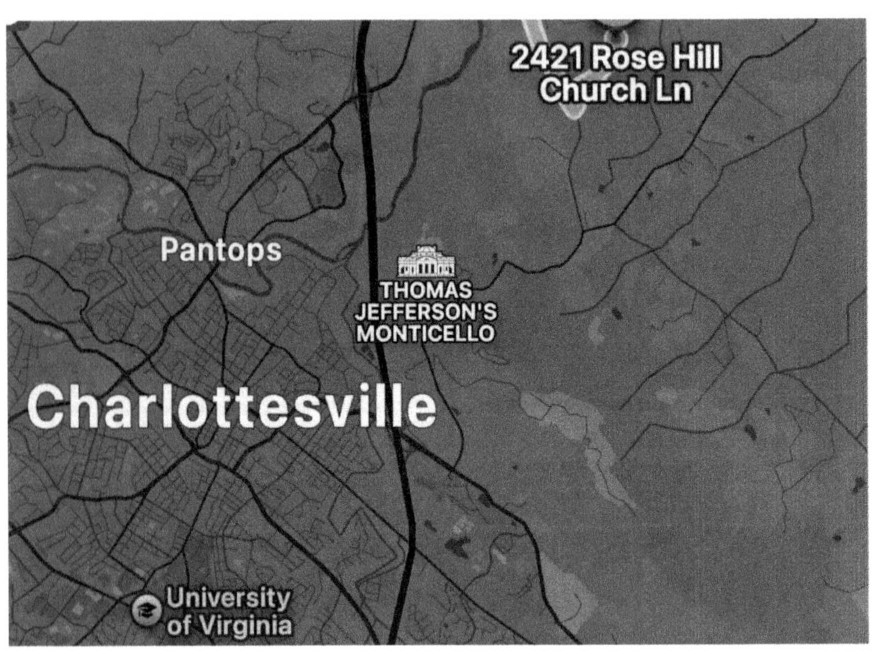
2421 Rose Hill
Church Ln
Pantops
THOMAS
JEFFERSON'S
MONTICELLO
Charlottesville
University
of Virginia

September 9, 1895   *August 1, 1970*

CHARLES ANDREW SAMPSON

*Gone but not forgotten. You represented
A consummate gentleman who loved his family.
You were a ray of light for every member of your family.
We missed your unusual humor, your
Witty jokes and most of all your warm since of family that
Only you could exhibit. To this day we share remembrances
Of the wonderful jesters of loved you shared with everyone
You met- friend, stranger, and most of all your impeccable love
Of family. While you are gone from us in the flesh, you are
For ever present in our lives through conversation, family
Gatherings and most of all your presence is felt in the place you
Called home.   We wait for the gathering of the saints where we
Will see you again in that cabin in the sky. God keep you in perfect
PEACE!*

*The Family
Daisy S. Moore and Carrie Juanita Sampson, daughters
George M. Moore, James E. Moore, Brenda D. Chappell, and Wiley A. Davis,III
Grand children
Keith Henery, Nicole Davis, Wiley A. Davis, IV- Great Grand children
Ghabriel James Davis, Great,Great Grand child, a host of other family and
FRIENDS.*

FRANK SAMPSON

May 20, 1904   *May 20, 1978*

*The Lord is my shepherd; I shall not want. He
maketh me to lie down in green pastures: he leadeth me
beside the still waters. He restoreth my soul: he leadeth
me in the paths of righteousness for His name's sake.
Yea, though I walk through the valley of the shadow of
death, I will fear no evil: for thou art with me; thy rod
and thy staff they comfort me. Thou preparest a table
before me in the presence of mine enemies,: thou
anointest my head with oil; my cup runneth over. Surely
goodness and mercy shall follow me all the days of my
life: and I will dwell in the house of the Lord for ever.*

In memory,
Daisy S. Moore, Carrie Juanita Sampson
&
The Family

Honoring
Pauline Sampson Davis
August 25, 1926 - May 28, 2003

Those we love must someday pass
beyond our present sight...
must leave us and the world we know
without their radiant light.
But we know that like a candle
their lovely light will shine
to brighten up another place
more perfect...more divine.

The Family
Brenda D. Chappell and Wiley A. Davis III

Grand Children
Keith Henery, Nicole Davis and Wiley IV

Great Grand Child
Ghabriel James Davis

*IN HONOR
Of
JANIE PROFFIT SAMPSON*

*The Rose is such a tender plant
And needs much loving care
With this twill grow in simple soil
And flourish anywhere.*

*A Rose is such a perfect flower
God sent His gentle touch
To brighten up a lonely spot
For one we love so much.*

*Our life is like a little Rose
We see it bloom and fall
He made our life, He made a Rose
The most perfect gifts of all.*

The Family

*Daisy S. Moore, Carrie Juanita Sampson, daughters
George M. Moore, James E. Moore, Brenda D. Chappell, Paul A. Davis
Grand Children
Many other relative and friends*

In Loving Memory of Mabel Proffit Sampson

February 12, 1907
February 12, 1995

"Oh, how blessed is the promise, When our soul is set free. To be absent from the body, Means to live, O Lord with Thee".

The Sampson Family
Daisy S. Moore, Carrie Juanita Sampson

George M. Moore, James E. Moore, Brenda D. Chappell,
Wiley A. Davis III, Keith Henery, Toyia Henery, Nicole Davis,
Wiley A. Davis IV
A host of other family and friends

Sometimes when life is lonely, we turn back the pages of time. There is joy in turning these pages. For to these sweet memories are final. Our Love for all of you will live in our hearts
Forever.

IN LOVING MEMORY

OF

DAISY SAMPSON SMITH

1910-1998

Lillie S. Calloway, daughter
A host of family and friends

In Loving Memory
Of

Charles Alexander Moore

We did not have the chance to say good-bye, but we know that God had a greater work for you. You are missed each and every day. We know that we will see you again in that great land in the sky. Rest in peace. We await the reunion in that heavenly kingdom.

The Family
Daisy S. Moore, mother, Phyllis Davis Moore, wife
George M. Moore and James E. Moore, brothers Carrie Juanita Sampson, aunt
and a host of other relative and friends.

IN LOVING MEMORY
Rosa Sampson Peterson
The Family
Oscar, Gladys, twins Edgar and Isabel, Ruth and Emery
Twelve grand children and thirty great-grand children
(photo- Rosa Sampson Peterson with youngest son Emery and his wife
Martha, and her youngest daughter Ruth)

In loving memory of our Grandparents

Fannie Thomas Sampson and Richard Sampson

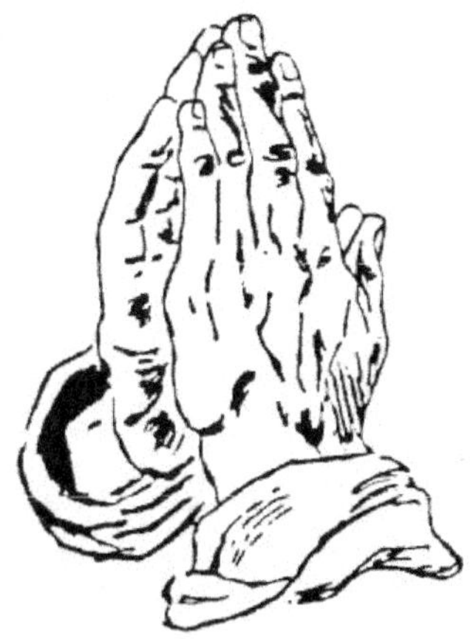

"When our life on earth is ended
And we reached the other shore
We shall meet our own dear loved ones
Who have gone that way before."

Grand daughters: Reva Sampson Crenshaw, and Grace Sampson
and the Great Grand Children

**Justice, Redemption, and the Untold Story of a Family
Connected to Monticello
I Ain't Goin' To Jail: Pardon Me?
By Hugh Carter**

In this powerful memoir and historical investigation, Hugh Carter recounts an extraordinary journey of justice, redemption, and ancestral discovery.

After serving a seven-year prison sentence and receiving a Governor's pardon more than three decades later, Carter begins exploring a deeper question: Where did my story really begin?

That search leads him to Virginia and to the historic mountain estate of Monticello, where his ancestor Eliza Tolliver Coleman served as a gatekeeper for more than forty years.

Through genealogical research, family records, and long-preserved oral history, Carter uncovers a remarkable lineage connecting the Coleman, Sampson, Harris, Smith, and Carter families to the landscape surrounding Monticello.

The journey deepens during a 1994 Sampson family reunion in Charlottesville, where relatives entrusted him with documents and a challenge: one day someone should write the family's story.

This book fulfills that promise.

Part memoir, part historical narrative, and part genealogical record, I Ain't Goin' To Jail: Pardon Me? reveals how one man's search for justice became a journey into the hidden history of a family whose roots stretch from the gates of Monticello to land they built and called their own in Simeon, Virginia. It is a story of resilience, memory, and the enduring power of family history.

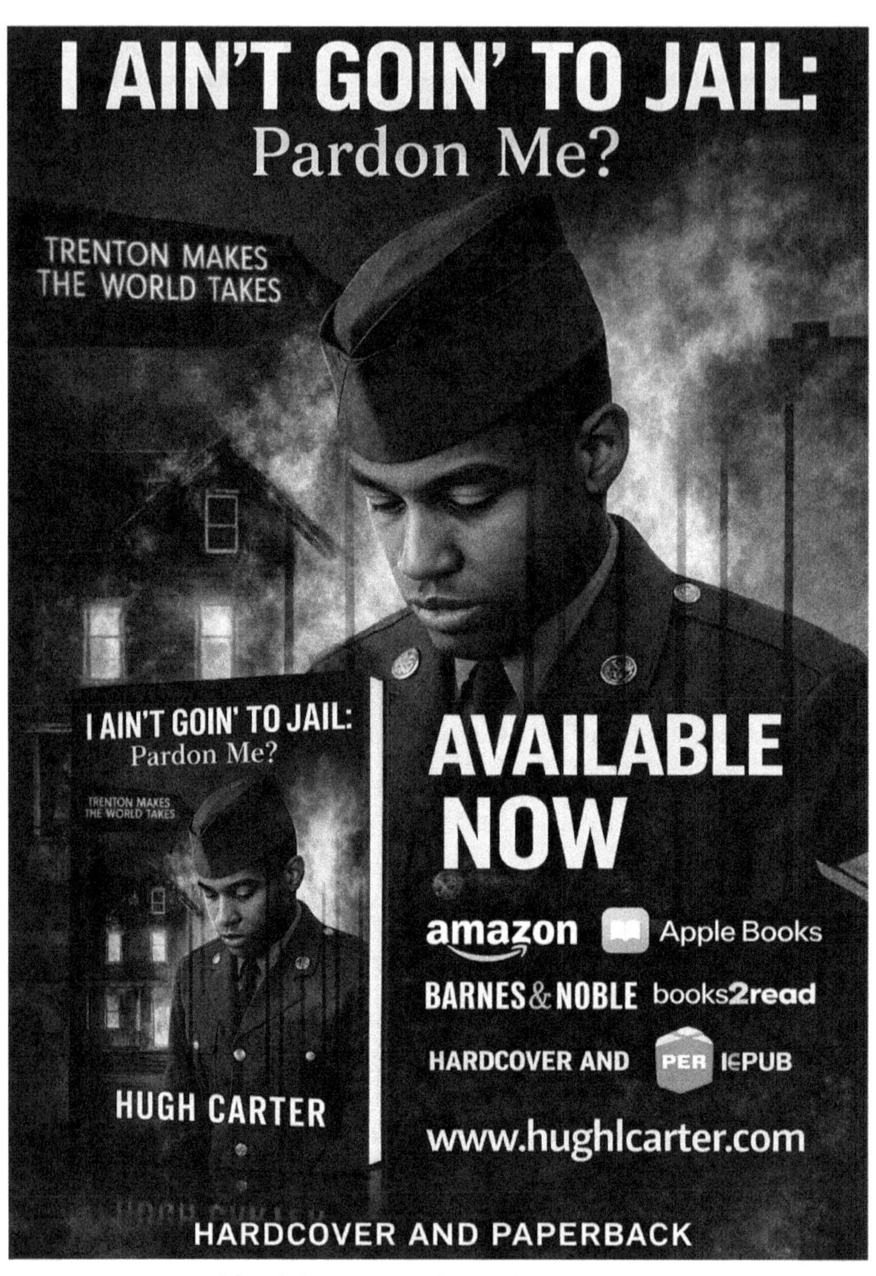

My debut memoir available now!

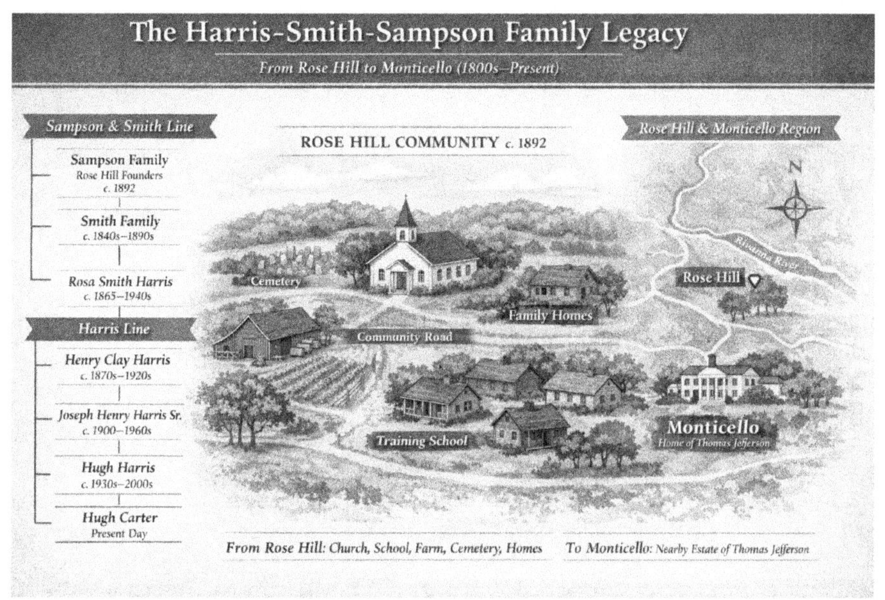

For Illustration Purpose not Proximate.

Chapter Seven — Rose Hill: The Land our Family Built

Just two miles south of Monticello lies the rural community of Simeon, Virginia. In this quiet landscape of rolling hills and fertile farmland stood a place that would become central to the story of our family: Rose Hill.

Rose Hill was more than land. It was the place where formerly enslaved families and their descendants began to build lives of independence, faith, and community after generations of bondage. Among those families were the descendants of Eliza Tolliver Coleman and the Sampson family, whose story became deeply woven into the fabric of the region.

At the center of that story stood two remarkable people remembered by generations simply as Papa and Mama Sampson: Charles Sampson and Laura Sampson.

Their lives represented a turning point in the family's history — the transition from tenant labor and uncertainty to land ownership, stability, and community leadership.

The Search for Our African Heritage

For many years, members of our family have searched for answers about our deeper origins.

Like many African American families whose ancestors lived through slavery, much of the earlier record was lost, hidden, or never written down. Yet the desire to understand where we came from has remained strong.

Family members have often spoken about the hope of discovering our African roots — identifying the tribes, clans, or regions from which our ancestors may have come before being brought to America.

This search continues today.

Research has revealed that Charles Sampson, whom the family affectionately called Papa Sampson, was born in Fluvanna County, Virginia. His parentage remains uncertain, and the historical record has yet to reveal who his parents were.

His wife, Laura Sampson, known within the family as Mama Sampson, is believed to have been born in Albemarle County, Virginia. Her mother was remembered by family members as Cornelia Shepherd.

One of the most important memories passed down through the family came from Aunt Daisy Smith, who recalled that her grandmother Cornelia Shepherd once lived with a relative known as Aunt Willie.

These fragments of memory became clues in the ongoing search to reconstruct the family's deeper history.

Even today, members of the extended Sampson family continue researching, hoping to uncover the missing links that connect the present generation with those who came

before.

A Family of Faith and Strength

Those who knew Papa and Mama Sampson often spoke of them with admiration and respect.

They were remembered as a deeply spiritual couple who raised their children to pursue high ideals and strong moral values.

In the Rose Hill community, they were seen as pillars of stability and leadership.

Their home stood on the highest hill in the Rose Hill community.

It was the largest house in the area and sat beneath a massive oak tree that shaded the front lawn. From that hillone could see much of the surrounding farmland.

The Sampson farm became one of the largest in Albemarle County.

People traveled from miles around to purchase livestock, produce, and other goods from the farm. Papa Sampson raised animals and crops that helped supply the surrounding community, and his success became well known in the region.

Despite the challenges of the era, poverty never defined the Sampson household. Hard work, careful stewardship of land, and a strong sense of faith created stability for the family.

Life at Tufton

Before they owned their land at Rose Hill, Charles and Laura Sampson lived at a place known as Tufton.

Tufton had originally been owned by Martha Jefferson Randolph, who received the property from her father, Thomas Jefferson.

During that time, much of the surrounding land in Albemarle County had once been connected to Jefferson's estates.

The Sampsons lived and worked at Tufton as tenant farmers or sharecroppers, a common arrangement for many families during that period.

The tenants working the land came from many backgrounds. Some were Black families and some were white families. Most were there for the same reason: to earn enough money to eventually purchase land of their own.

According to family recollections, the people working the land often lived similar lives.

They prayed together.
They worked the land together.
They sought what little education they could obtain together.

Among those families there was often less emphasis on racial hierarchy than on survival and shared struggle.

Building the Rose Hill Farm

When Charles and Laura Sampson finally accumulated enough money, they purchased land at Rose Hill.

That moment marked a major turning point in the family's history.

Owning land represented freedom, independence, and security for future generations.

After purchasing the property, Papa Sampson began clearing the land.

Trees were cut and shaped by hand. Lumber was prepared for the construction of the family home.

When it came time to build, neighbors came together to help raise the structure. This type of community effort was

common in rural Virginia, where families relied on one another to accomplish large tasks.

Soon the Sampson family moved into their new home.

They brought with them cattle, chickens, pigs, and seeds for planting crops. From that foundation they began

building a successful farm.

A Self-Sustaining Household

The Sampson farm was largely self-sufficient.

Most of what the family ate came directly from the land.

Laura Sampson managed the household garden and cared for the chickens while also supervising the

preparation and preservation of food.

Children and neighbors often helped gather berries used to make jams and jellies. Vegetables were canned and

stored for the winter months.
Laura also made clothing for the family.

Sheets, quilts, bedspreads, and garments were sewn at home.

The household owned several items that were considered luxuries for the time:

• a sewing machine
• an organ
• a Victrola
• electric lighting powered by a small motor

The presence of these items reflected the success and stability the family had achieved.

Good Times

Food was a central part of life on the farm.

**Breakfast might include: fried apples sausage
side meat
batter bread
eggs**

Dinner, which was served around two in the afternoon, was the main meal of the day. It often included stews or gumbo along with several vegetables.

Meats varied depending on what was available. The family raised pork and beef but also hunted wild game such as rabbit, squirrel, groundhog, raccoon, and occasionally deer.

Meals were accompanied by cornbread, hoe cakes, or hot rolls.

Supper was usually lighter, often including pies or cakes along with bread, milk, and butter.

On Sundays the midday meal was special. The preacher and his wife frequently joined the family for dinner.

Sunday meals might include fried chicken, ham, roast beef, corn pudding, fresh vegetables, mashed potatoes, and homemade desserts.

Work and Community Life

The Sampson farm required the labor of many people.

Men worked in the fields growing crops and managing livestock. Women worked in the household, prepared meals, and preserved food for the seasons ahead.

The midday meal during the work week was especially large because the family needed to feed the workers who labored on the farm.

Life was busy, but the work built a thriving agricultural enterprise.

Faith at the Center of the Home

No matter how tired the family was at the end of the day, they always gathered for prayer.

Evenings included:
Bible reading
prayer
singing hymns together

Charles Sampson sometimes played the accordion as the family sang.

After prayers everyone said their good nights and prepared for the next day's work.

Faith, family, and discipline formed the foundation of the household.

A Legacy That Endures

The story of Charles and Laura Sampson represents the determination of a generation that moved from the shadow of slavery into a life of independence through land ownership, faith, and community.

Their descendants spread across the region, but the legacy of Rose Hill remains.

The land they built continues to hold deep meaning for the generations that followed.

And for those who carry the Sampson name and heritage, Rose Hill is not just a place on a map.

It is home.

Family Tree
The Coleman–Sampson–Harris Lineage Foundational
Generation — Slavery Era
Grace Coleman Harris
(Enslaved woman connected to the Monticello region)
↓
Eliza Tolliver Coleman
Born into slavery in Albemarle County, Virginia Associated with the plantations surrounding Monticello
↓
Early Coleman Descendants
Families emerging from slavery into Reconstruction-era Virginia
↓
The Sampson Family Line
Charles "Papa" Sampson Born in Fluvanna County, Virginia married
Laura "Mama" Sampson
Daughter of Cornelia Sheppard of Albemarle County
↓

Children of Charles and Laura Sampson
Early descendants born at Tufton Farm, later moving to Rose Hill.
↓
The Rose Hill Generation
Sampson descendants who helped build the Rose Hill community in Simeon, Virginia.
Institutions connected to the family community include:
• Rose Hill Baptist Church
• Albemarle Training School
Both Black and white families worked and studied together in this rural community.
↓
Modern Descendants
Generations carrying forward the family legacy of:
Faith
Land ownership Education Community leadership
↓
Hugh Carter
Author, Army Veteran, and descendant of the Coleman–Sampson lineage preserving this history.

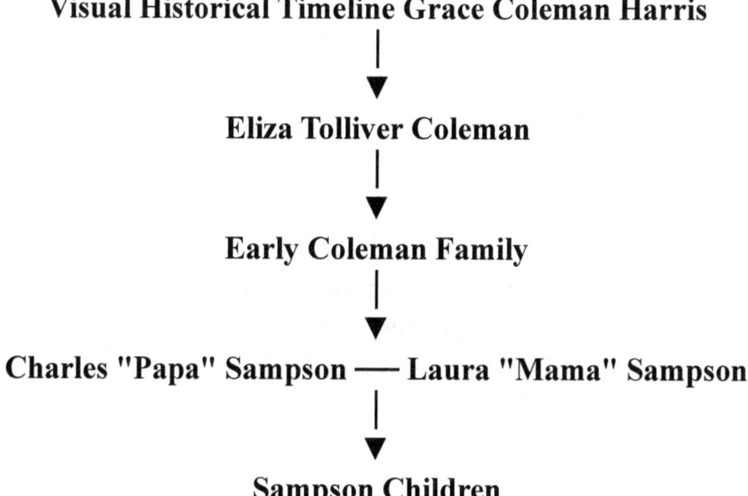

Visual Historical Timeline Grace Coleman Harris
Eliza Tolliver Coleman
Early Coleman Family
Charles "Papa" Sampson —— Laura "Mama" Sampson
Sampson Children

▼

Rose Hill Community Generation
|
▼

Modern Descendants
|
▼

Hugh Carter
From Slavery to Land Ownership
1700s–1865
Slavery in Albemarle County

African Americans including ancestors of the Coleman line lived and worked on plantations surrounding Monticello.
Enslaved families built the agricultural wealth of the region while struggling to preserve their family identity.
1865 Emancipation
After the Civil War, formerly enslaved families began searching for ways to survive as free citizens.
Many worked as tenant farmers or sharecroppers on the same land where they had once been enslaved.
Late 1800s
Life at Tufton
The Sampson family worked at Tufton Farm, originally associated with the Jefferson family through Martha Jefferson Randolph.
Families working the land included both Black and white farmers striving to eventually purchase land of their own.
Late 1800s – Early 1900s The Purchase of Rose Hill
Charles and Laura Sampson accumulated enough money to purchase land at Rose Hill in Simeon, Virginia.
They cleared the land, built their home, and established one of the largest farms in the region.
Early 1900s
Building the Rose Hill Community

The community grew around institutions including:
• Rose Hill Baptist Church
• Albemarle Training School
The area became a thriving rural community where families
worshipped, studied, and worked together.

1994

The Sampson Family Reunion

At the first major Sampson family reunion, Hugh Carter's aunts and relatives welcomed him and presented a package of family history documents.

Family members encouraged someone to write the history of the Sampson family and the Rose Hill community.

Hugh Carter promised he would one day write that book.

Present Day
The Descendants Return to the Mountain
More than a century after Charles and Laura Sampson built their home at Rose Hill, their descendants continue researching the family's history.
The story of the Coleman–Sampson family reflects a powerful journey:
Slavery
→ Freedom
→ Land ownership
→ Community building → Historical preservation

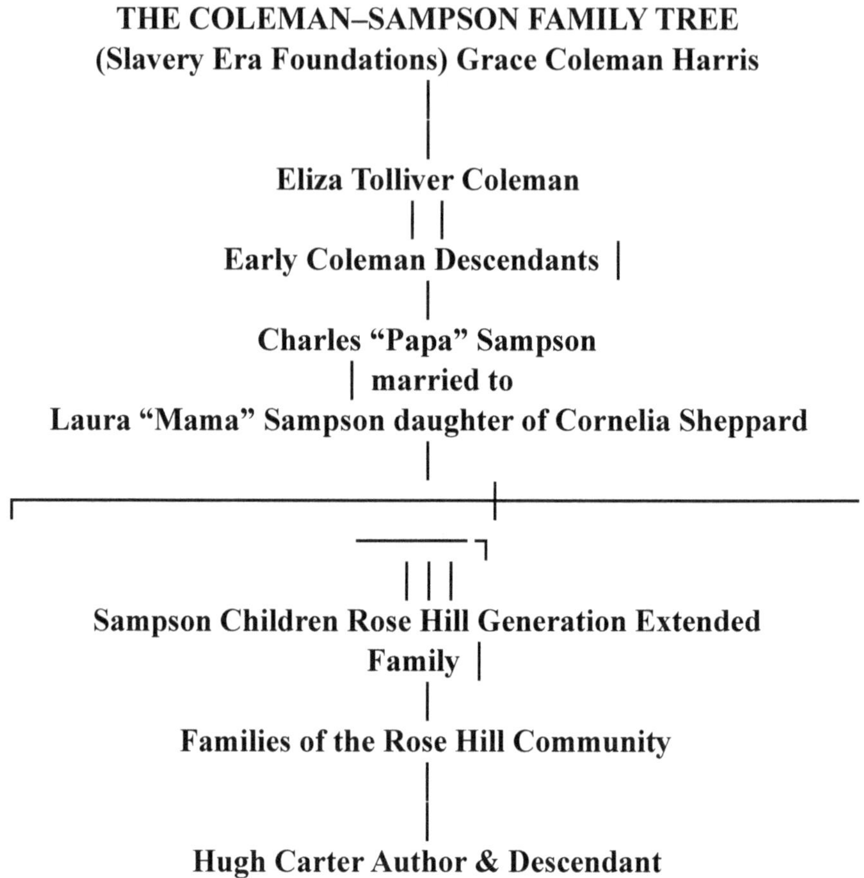

THE COLEMAN–SAMPSON FAMILY TREE
(Slavery Era Foundations) Grace Coleman Harris
Eliza Tolliver Coleman
Early Coleman Descendants
Charles "Papa" Sampson
married to
Laura "Mama" Sampson daughter of Cornelia Sheppard
Sampson Children Rose Hill Generation Extended Family
Families of the Rose Hill Community
Hugh Carter Author & Descendant

**Historical connection to
Monticello**

Community institutions connected to the family:

• Rose Hill Baptist Church • Albemarle Training School

Monticello to Rose Hill

This would appear like an 1800s surveyor map.

Map Title

**"The Sampson Family Landscape of Albemarle County,
Virginia"**

Map Landmarks 📍 Monticello

Center of early regional history.

↓

📍 Tufton Farm

**Location where Charles and Laura Sampson worked as
tenant farmers.**

↓

📍 Simeon

Rural crossroads where the Rose Hill community developed.

↓

**📍 Rose Hill Baptist Church Spiritual center of the Rose Hill
community.**

↓

📍 Albemarle Training School

**Education center attended by both Black and white students
in the community.**

Infographic Timeline
1700s–1865
Slavery in Albemarle County
African American ancestors including members of the Coleman lineage lived and worked on plantations surrounding Monticello.
1865
Freedom After the Civil War
Formerly enslaved families began building independent lives, often as tenant farmers or sharecroppers.
Late 1800s Life at Tufton
Charles Sampson and Laura Sampson lived and worked at Tufton Farm.
Families there included both Black and white farmers working to purchase their own land.
Late 1800s – Early 1900s
The Rose Hill Purchase
The Sampson family purchased land in the Simeon community and began clearing the land to build their farm.
Early 1900s

Building a Community
The Rose Hill area developed with churches, farms, and schools including:
• Rose Hill Baptist Church • Albemarle Training School

Harris Family Reunion 2004

Cousin Barbara Ann

1994 The Sampson Family Reunion

Family members gathered and shared historical documents, encouraging someone in the family to write the story of Rose Hill and the Sampson legacy.

Hugh Carter accepted that challenge.
Present Day Preserving the Legacy

1994

Descendants continue researching the Coleman and Sampson family history and preserving the legacy of Rose Hill for future generations.

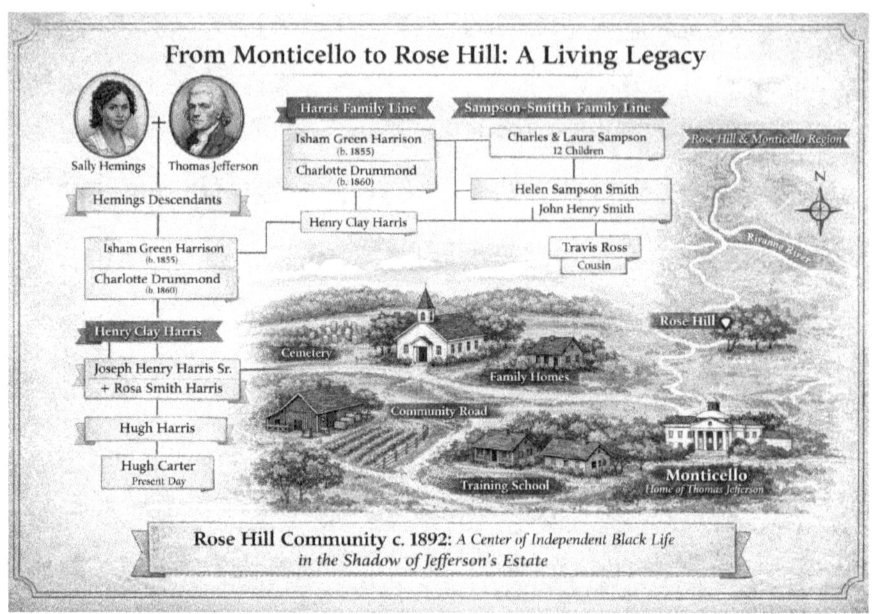

Image for illustration purposes.

Chapter Eight — From Monticello to Rosehill: A Living Legacy

For generations, the gates surrounding the estates and farms of Albemarle County symbolized more than property lines. They represented boundaries of opportunity, freedom, and belonging.Near the historic grounds of Monticello stood a gatehouse that controlled who could enter and who could not. These gates were designed to protect the estates of powerful landowners, but they also reflected the deeper divisions that shaped American history.

For African Americans whose ancestors had lived and worked on these lands, the gates carried a different meaning. They reminded families of generations who had labored within those boundaries while denied ownership, recognition, and the rights that others enjoyed.

Yet behind those gates lived stories that could never be contained by property lines.

Families like the Colemans and the Sampsons built lives rooted in faith, hard work, and community. Even during the years when opportunity was restricted, they created institutions that strengthened the people around them.

One of those institutions was the church.

The building of Rose Hill Baptist Church became a cornerstone of the Rose Hill community. The church stood not only as a place of worship but also as a gathering place where families organized, learned, and supported one another.

Education also played a critical role in shaping the future.

Children from the Rose Hill area attended the historic Albemarle Training School. In an unusual dynamic for the time, both Black and white students shared parts of the educational experience in the rural farming community.

Inside the gates of farms and communities like Rose Hill, people built lives that demonstrated resilience. They grew crops, raised families, built homes, and established traditions that would survive long after the physical gates themselves faded.

The gates may have marked boundaries on the land, but they could never contain the spirit of the people who lived there.

"The Rose Hill community held more than memories— it held our dead. Public land records and family death certificates confirm that a burial ground existed there where generations of the Smith family were laid to rest, including my great-grandmother Helen Louise Smith. What remained of the cemetery stood as quiet testimony to the lives of African American families connected to the Monticello region."

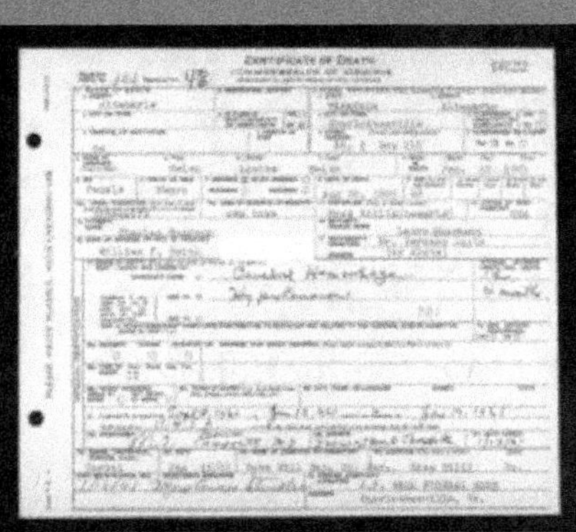

Photo added by Tosh13

Helen Louise *Sampson* Smith

BIRTH 20 Aug 1892
Rose Hill, Albemarle County, Virginia, USA

DEATH 10 Jan 1961 (aged 68)
Albemarle County, Virginia, USA

BURIAL Rose Hill Cemetery
Milton, Albemarle County, Virginia, USA

Harris Family Reunion 2005

Harris Family Reunion 2004

My Dad Hugh Harris

Me and my mom and nephews

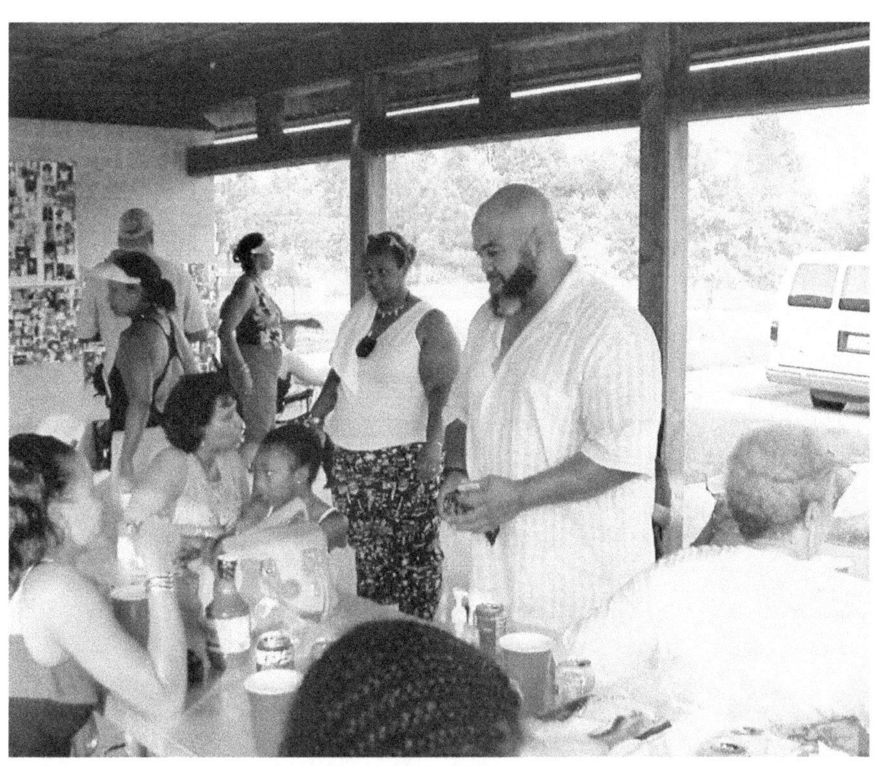

Brother Kevin Brian Harris at 2004 Harris Family Reunion

Family Reunion 2004

Sampson Family Reunion 2007 Washington D.C.

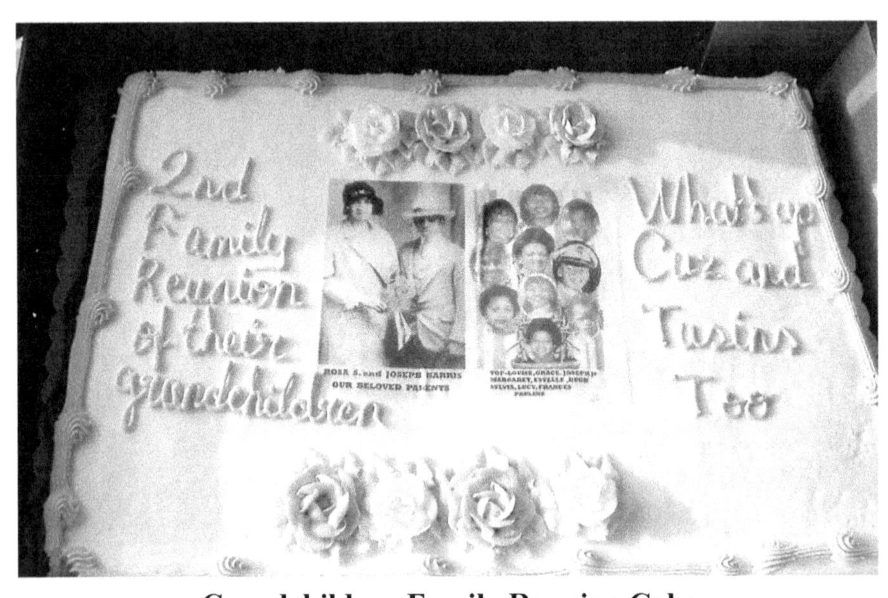

Grandchildren Family Reunion Cake

The story of my family cannot be told without acknowledging the deep and complex history of Monticello. Through Grace Coleman Harris, my ancestry traces directly to the Hemings family, descendants of Sally Hemings, and thus to Thomas Jefferson himself. This connection is not simply a genealogical curiosity—it is a living thread that ties my lineage to the very heart of American history.

Grace Coleman Harris was a bridge between worlds. While her ancestors endured the hardships of enslavement at Monticello, she represents a continuation of life, survival, and agency. Her story is mirrored in the lives of those who would go on to build communities like Rose Hill. In 1892, members of the Sampson and Smith families established this settlement, purchasing land to build homes, a farm, a church, a training school, and a cemetery. It was a community deliberately constructed to provide work, education, and spiritual nourishment, ensuring that future generations could thrive outside the shadow of the plantation.

My father's mother, Rosa Smith Harris, was born into this lineage. She carried forward the strength and independence of the Rose Hill founders and married into the Harris family. Their son, Joseph Henry Harris Sr., and my father, Hugh Harris, inherited not only the family name but also the enduring legacy of resilience and community leadership.

Through them, the story of Rose Hill remains connected to the larger history of Monticello's enslaved families.

The juxtaposition is striking. While Thomas Jefferson's estate is remembered for grandeur, politics, and architectural legacy, Rose Hill tells another story—of ordinary people who labored, built, and educated themselves to survive and thrive. Through Grace Coleman Harris, my lineage connects these two worlds: the enslaved families at Monticello and the independent Black communities that rose from the ashes of slavery.

Understanding this connection transforms history from a distant, static record into a living narrative. It is not just a story of Jefferson or Monticello; it is my story, my family's story, and the story of every descendant who walks in the footsteps of those who endured, resisted, and built legacies that would survive long after the gates of the estate closed.

This living connection also provides a tangible framework for exploring the lives of the Colemans and other families whose names are recorded only sporadically in Monticello's plantation records. Many enslaved men and women appear without surnames, identified only by first names.

Through oral history and family documentation, we can trace how these individuals' descendants—like Grace Coleman Harris—played pivotal roles in building self- sustaining communities like Rose Hill. They created schools, churches, and farms that became the lifeblood of post-emancipation African American society.

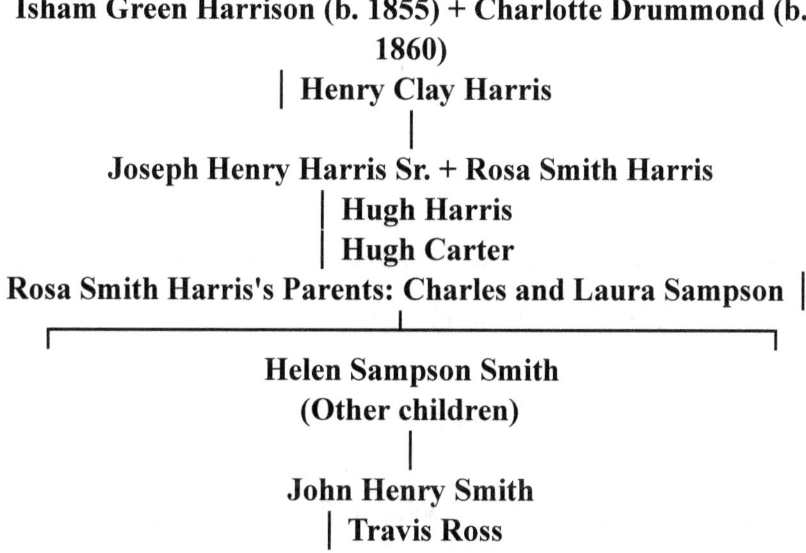

In Rose Hill, the legacy of Monticello is not forgotten; it is transformed. The cemetery holds the remains of my great-grandmother, Helen Louise Smith, and her brother, a World War I veteran, demonstrating the continuity of family, faith, and service across generations. Every home, field, and building in Rose Hill embodies the determination of my ancestors to live fully outside the constraints of the gates, and it reminds me that our family story is inseparable from the broader story of African Americans in Virginia —from slavery to freedom, from survival to self-determination.

The Eppes family was part of the powerful planter class in colonial Virginia and was closely tied to Jefferson

through marriage and kinship.

- **John Wayles Eppes married Jefferson's daughter in 1797.**

- **The family owned large plantations and enslaved laborers.**

The wealth of such planter families came largely from land ownership and enslaved labor in tobacco and agricultural production, which dominated Virginia's plantation economy.

During the height of plantation operations, 100–125 enslaved people lived and worked at Monticello, and Jefferson enslaved roughly 600 people throughout his lifetime across his various properties.

Many enslaved families—such as the Hemings family— had complicated relationships with Jefferson's extended family network through ownership, inheritance, and intermarriage among elite Virginia planter families.

"Even if the gates of history were once closed to our story, the land records, graves, and memories remain."

Sally Hemings + Thomas Jefferson |
Hemings Descendants Coleman Family |
Grace Coleman Harris Rosa Smith Harris |
Joseph Henry Harris Sr. Hugh Harris |
Hugh Carter
| |
|

Rose Hill Community (Founded c.1892)
| Sampson Family
|

Smith Family |
Rosa Smith Harris |
Joseph Henry Harris Sr. |
Hugh Harris |
Hugh Carter

Family Time Line

Spouse and Children   Parents and Siblings

1820   1840   1860   1880   1900   1920   1940   1960   1980   2000

 Thomas Coleman   1845–Deceased

 Eliza Tolliver   1845–1932

 Lewis B. Coleman   1865–Deceased

 Lucy Coleman Page   1867–1957

 Louisa Coleman twin   1867–Deceased

 Douglass Coleman   1871–1935

 Phillip Coleman   1874–Deceased

 Susan Ellen Coleman   1876–1947

 Paul Coleman   1878–1936

 Grace Coleman   1879–1947

 Susie Allen Coleman   1879–1963

Laura Shepard family tree

(i) Family tree · Create your own family tree

Parents

Robert Shepard
1850 - Unknown

Cornelia Morris
1850 - Unknown

Spouse(s)

Charles Edward Sampson
1862 - 1936

Children   Show all

Selton Sampson
1900 - 1928

Hampton Sonyson
1897 - 1940

Daisy Sampson
1910 - 1998

Rosa Sampson
1884 - 1960

Parents and Siblings

Isham Green Harrison
1855–Deceased

Charlotte Drummond
1860–1937

Siblings (9)

Louisa Ida Harrison
1877–1938

Henry Clay Harris
1878–1970

George Harrison
1880–Deceased

Lucy Jane Harrison
1880–1934

Matilda A. Harrison
1880–Deceased

+4 More Children

Family Time Line

Spouse and Children | **Parents and Siblings**

1840 1860 1880 1900 1920 1940 1960 1980 2000

Charles Sampson 1862–Deceased

Laura Smith 1869–1947

Rosa Sampson 1884–Deceased

Sutton Sampson 1901–1928

Jacob Sampson 1891–1963

Helen Louise Sampson 1892–1961

Charlie Sampson 1892–Deceased

Lena Sampson 1893–1948

Charles Andrew Sampson 1894–1970

Hampton Sampson 1897–Deceased

Selton Sampson 1899–Deceased

Selton Sampson 1900–1928

Robert Sampson 1904–1987

Frank L Sampson 1904–1975

Cornelia Sampson 1905–Deceased

Frank Sampson 1908–1975

Daisy Sampson 1908–1998

Spouse and Children

Henry Clay Harris
1878–1970

Grace Coleman
1879–1947

Marriage
20 December 1898
Albemarle, Virginia, United States

Children (5)

Louise A Harris
1902–1979

Joseph Henry Harris
1903–1945

Virginia A Harris
1905–Deceased

Martha E Harris
1907–Deceased

Samuel C Harris
1910–1962

VIEW ALL

Parents and Siblings

Isham Green Harrison
1855–Deceased

Charlotte Drummond
1860–1937

Family Time Line

Spouse and Children   Parents and Siblings

1880   1900   1920   1940   1960   1980   2000   2020   2040

 **Joseph Henry Harris**   1903–1945

 Rosa Anna Smith   1909–1955

 Marriage: 8 December 1926

 Louise Harris   1927–1983

 Grace Harris   1930–Deceased

 Frances Victoria Harris   1943–1955

 Pauline Doris Harris   1944–2001

Charles Andrew Sampson

2 September 1894–1 Augu... •G4QG-3XM

Brief Life History of Charles Andrew

When Charles Andrew Sampson was born on 2 September 1894, in Albemarle, Virginia, United States, his father, Charles Sampson, was 32 and his mother, Laura Smith, was 24. He married Janie E Proffitt on 4 March 1925, in Charlottesville, Virginia, United States. They were the parents of at least 2 daughters. He lived in Rivanna, Albemarle, Virginia, United States for about 10 years and Virginia, United States in 1950. He registered for military service in 1919. He died on 1 August 1970, in Keswick, Albemarle, Virginia, United States, at the age o...

Brief Life History of Joseph Henry

When Joseph Henry Harris was born in 1903, in Virginia, United States, his father, Henry Clay Harris, was 25 and his mother, Grace Coleman, was 24. He married Rosa Anna Smith on 8 December 1926, in Manhattan, New York City, New York, United States. They were the parents of at least 4 daughters. He lived in Manhattan, New York City, New York, United States in 1930 and Scottsville District, Albemarle, Virginia, United States in 1940. He died on 30 November 1945, in Fife Family Cemetery, Albemarle, Virginia, United States, at the age of 42.

Brief Life History of Louise

When Louise Harris was born on 1 December 1927, in New York City, New York, United States, her father, Joseph Henry Harris, was 24 and her mother, Rosa Anna Smith, was 18. She married Samuel Lee Fernandez on 10 October 1959, in Boston, Suffolk, Massachusetts, United States. She lived in New York, United States in 1935 and Scottsville District, Albemarle, Virginia, United States in 1940. She died on 17 January 1983, in Princeton, Mercer, New Jersey, United States, at the age of 55.

Ozella Harvey and four other descendants of Monticello gatekeeper Eliza Tolliver Coleman were interviewed together in 1995. All live in the Washington, DC, area and work (or worked) in various departments of the federal government. They shared their memories of Eliza Coleman's daughters Lucy Coleman Barnaby Page and Grace Coleman Harris and recalled summers spent at the Monticello gatehouse. Members of the extended Coleman family lived at Monticello for more than a century—far longer than any of the property's owners.

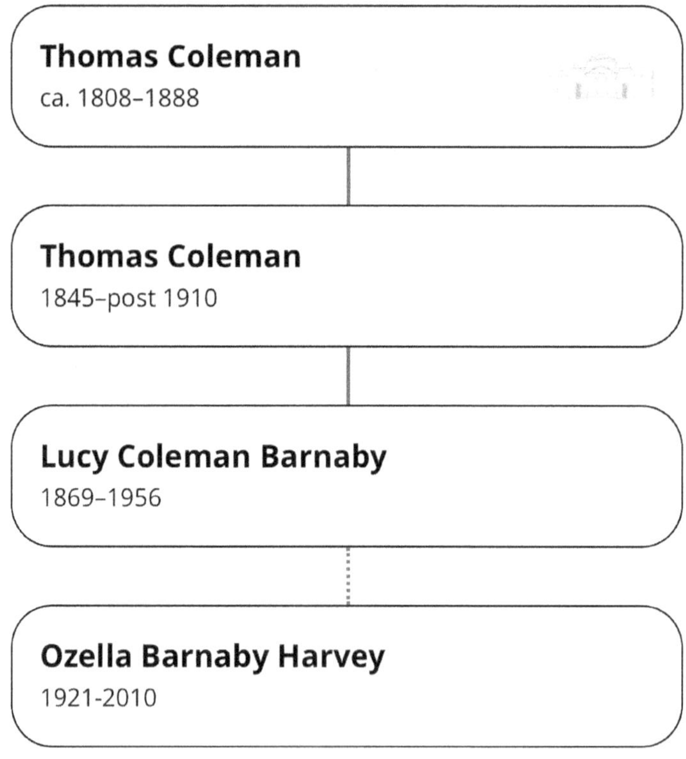

Colbert

Betty Brown, the second daughter of Elizabeth Hemings, had eight children, six of whom used the surname Colbert; their father has not been identified. Her son Burwell Colbert was Jefferson's valued enslaved manservant in his retirement years as well as Monticello butler; he was also a painter and glazier. The descendants of his daughter Nancy Colbert Scott preserve an oral history of their ancestors that presents a striking portrait of the evils of slavery.

Betty Brown's daughter Melinda Colbert married John Freeman, Jefferson's dining-room servant at the President's House; they raised a family in freedom in Washington, DC, and were active in antislavery activities there. Two of their grandsons distinguished themselves in the Union army in the Civil War. Melinda's brother Robert Colbert was sold by Jefferson in 1820 and subsequently ran away; he was described in an advertisement as being "shrewd and intelligent" and having "somewhat" the appearance of an Indian. His fate is not known.

Another of Betty Brown's sons, Brown Colbert, was an enslaved nailmaker at Monticello. To prevent separation from his wife, he asked Jefferson to sell him in 1805. With his wife and family, he lived in slavery in Lexington, Virginia, but was able to remain in contact with his mother and siblings at Monticello and in Washington. Surviving records indicate that this family made extraordinary efforts to maintain family bonds despite separation and to support their family members, both free and enslaved. While Brown Colbert's bid for freedom in 1833 ended in tragedy on the west coast of Africa, his children who remained in Virginia laid the groundwork for the success of their descendants, who were educators, civic leaders, and soldiers in the Civil War.

Nannie Cox Jackson

Burwell Colbert's receipt for purchases at 1827 Monticello sale (University of Virginia Library)

Brown Colbert's great-granddaughter Coralie Franklin Cook was a prominent lecturer and suffragist (West Virginia Archives)

All Sally Hemings family listed

Tracing my extended family brings even more connections to light. My father's mother, Rosa Smith Harris, was one of twelve children born to Charles and Laura Sampson. One of her sisters, Helen Sampson Smith, had a son named John Henry Smith, whose child is my cousin Travis Ross.

This network of cousins, siblings, and descendants highlights how the Sampson/Smith families shaped the Rose Hill community. They were not just neighbors—they were builders of farms, churches, schools, and cemeteries.

The bonds between these families sustained them across generations, preserving the memory of Monticello's enslaved families while creating institutions that nurtured independence, education, and community cohesion.

Through Rosa Smith Harris and her siblings, including Helen Sampson Smith, cousins like Travis Ross carry forward this shared legacy.

Together, our family story weaves through the post-emancipation era, into the thriving Rose Hill community, and into the present, showing that the history of resilience and self- determination is alive in every branch of our family tree.As I began tracing my father's family line, the names revealed a clearer path into the past. My father, Hugh Harris, was the son of Joseph Henry Harris Sr., whose father was Henry Clay Harris.

Through my father's mother, Rosa Smith Harris, the Harris family was connected to the Smith and Sampson families who helped build the Rose Hill community. That meant the story of Rose Hill was not a distant piece of history—it was part of my direct lineage.

Generations before I was born, families like the Sampsons and Smiths had built farms, homes, a church, and a training school on that land. Their work created a community that would sustain their descendants long after the plantation era had ended.

My aunt Sylvia Page Coles and her granddaughter Kodi at the gate in Monticello recently

Chapter Nine — Bloodlines, Land, and The Gate

If the gates kept some people inside, they also kept many things outside.

For much of American history, the gates of opportunity were closed to African Americans whose ancestors had helped build the nation's wealth through forced labor.

Even after emancipation, systems of inequality often prevented families from fully participating in the opportunities that others took for granted.

Land ownership, however, changed that story for many families.

When Charles "Papa" Sampson and Laura "Mama" Sampson purchased land at Rose Hill, they achieved something that many formerly enslaved families struggled to obtain: independence through property ownership.

Their success represented a quiet revolution.

Owning land meant stability. It meant control over one's labor and the ability to build wealth that could be passed down to future generations.

Yet many historical records failed to capture the achievements of families like the Sampsons.

While the estates of prominent figures were carefully documented and preserved, the stories of rural Black communities often remained scattered in family memories, church records, and oral histories.

The gates of history itself sometimes kept those stories out.

That absence is why preserving family history matters.

By documenting the lives of the Coleman and Sampson families, descendants ensure that their contributions to Albemarle County and the Rose Hill community are not forgotten.

History belongs not only to those who built grand estates but also to the families who built farms, churches, and communities with their own hands.

On the mountain where Monticello stands, history is layered like the soil beneath the vineyards. The house that the world associates with Thomas Jefferson was never built by one man alone.

Beneath its classical architecture and carefully measured symmetry lies the labor, lives, and bloodlines of hundreds of enslaved people.

Among those families connected to the mountain were the Colemans.

My research began with a simple fact recorded in oral history and preserved in fragments of local memory:

Thomas Coleman was an enslaved man connected to the Monticello community who later married Eliza Coleman, a woman whose life became inseparable from the mountain itself. After the Civil War, Eliza would become the gatekeeper at Monticello, greeting visitors who came to see Jefferson's estate long after the man himself had died.

Yet even as visitors passed through the gate she guarded, the deeper story of families like hers remained largely outside the narrative told to the public.

Descendants of the Coleman line have long repeated a quiet tradition —that Eliza Coleman "came out of that Jefferson tree." Historians have acknowledged the existence of that tradition while admitting that the exact connection has never been fully documented.

But Monticello's history itself suggests why such stories persist.

During Jefferson's lifetime, hundreds of enslaved people lived and worked on the plantation. They built the bricks, forged the nails, and carved the wood that shaped the house on the hill. They were carpenters, cooks, blacksmiths, gardeners, and field workers. Some families remained there for generations, forming a community whose lives were intertwined with the Jefferson household.

The complicated web of relationships among Virginia's planter families only deepened that entanglement.

One such family was the Eppes family, a powerful Virginia planter lineage that became directly connected to Jefferson through marriage. Jefferson's daughter married John Wayles Eppes, linking two influential families whose plantations stretched across large tracts of Virginia land. Wealth, political influence, and agricultural power flowed through these networks.

Plantation wealth in Virginia did not appear out of thin air. It was built through land speculation, enslaved labor, and global trade networks that connected the American colonies to Europe, the Caribbean, and Africa.

In that world, families like the Eppes were not only landowners but also participants in the economic systems that sustained slavery across the Atlantic world. Tobacco,

wheat, and other crops grown by enslaved labor fueled fortunes that financed estates, political careers, and architectural ambitions.

Jefferson himself was famously fascinated with architecture. Monticello was not built once but redesigned again and again over decades, reflecting Jefferson's obsession with classical design and European ideas.

Yet even Jefferson struggled financially. His estates, like those of many Virginia planters, were often burdened with debt.

That raises questions that historians continue to explore.

How were such ambitious architectural projects sustained?

Who truly financed the expansion of plantation estates?

And how many lives were bound to those projects through labor, inheritance, and enslavement?

Within that broader landscape, the story of the Colemans emerges
not simply as a footnote, but as a

reminder of the hidden communities that surrounded Monticello.

Eliza Coleman stood at the gate.

Visitors saw her as the woman who welcomed them to Jefferson's
mountain. But beyond that gate stretched generations of untold
history—families whose lives were shaped by the same land long
before tourists arrived to admire the house.

If Jefferson's world was defined by architecture, politics, and
philosophy, the world outside the gate was defined by endurance.
The Colemans lived there.

Worked there.

Raised their children there.

And in ways still being uncovered, their story may be more deeply
rooted in the history of Monticello than the official record has yet
revealed.

I felt that this was to important to leave out. Back in the 1980s, Rev. Herbert Townes and his wife, Emma, celebrated their wedding anniversary at a local Japanese steakhouse. They were the only African-Americans at a table otherwise occupied by people whose ancestors had come to the U.S. from different parts of Europe.

As the other diners introduced themselves one by one and recounted their families' origin stories, Townes thought, 'What am I going to say when they get to me? Where am I going to say I'm from?'"

He realized the answer was more complex than merely knowing his place of birth: the Hallsboro area of Chesterfield.

"I needed to know my homeland," Townes recalled during his Black History Month presentation, Slave Trading and the Early African American Presence in Bermuda Hundred, last Saturday at the Chesterfield County Museum.

"I'm a gardener," he added. "It's like a seed was planted in me and it kept being nurtured and cultivated by these different life experiences, longing to know where I was from, where in the motherland did my ancestors live?"

Townes visited the west coast of Africa and walked through "The Door of No Return" at two former slave castles, where enslaved people were held captive in dungeons until it was time to board a ship bound for North, Central or South America or the Caribbean.

It was called "The Door of No Return" because once an enslaved African walked through the door and got on the ship, they were never coming back.

About six years ago, Townes' existential journey came full circle at a small southeastern Chesterfield community known as Bermuda Hundred. Standing on the banks of the James River, he looked out at the remains of a wharf where slave ships once docked and unloaded scores of enslaved African people to be sold in the town square.

By that point, Townes had discovered his great- grandfather was born in Amelia County in 1842 and wanted to know how his family got there.

He wound up learning much more – namely that, for more than a quarter-century leading up to the start of the American Revolution, Bermuda Hundred functioned as Virginia's principal market for enslaved Africans.

"We hear a lot about the slave trade in Richmond, but in my research I was never able to find any advertisements for enslaved people being sold off ships that docked in Richmond. There were many for ships that landed at Bermuda Hundred," Townes said.

Founded by Sir Thomas Dale in 1613 at the confluence of the James and Appomattox rivers, Bermuda Hundred was the first British administrative division in the colony of Virginia.

From 1690 to 1775, white Virginians bought approximately 100,000 enslaved Africans from transatlantic slave traders. Ports at Bermuda Hundred and Osborne Landing dominated sales in the Richmond-Petersburg region.

An advertisement in the July 10, 1762 edition of the Virginia Gazette reads as follows: "Just arrived in James River from Old Callabar, the Anne Galley, Capt. Alexander Robe, with a cargo of choice healthy slaves, the sale of which will begin at Bermuda Hundred on Thursday the 16th and there be continued until all are sold."

Another ad from the same newspaper in September 1772 notes the arrival of the ship Prince of Wales with about 400 "fine, healthy slaves" to be sold at Bermuda Hundred.

Enslaved Africans were chained, stowed and stacked like cargo in the cramped, dark and filthy holds of ships.

Diseases ran rampant and the overall death rate was about 20%. Most of those who survived the harrowing voyage to Virginia were sold and marched to the Piedmont region, where planters utilized their labor in an expanding agricultural economy."It's almost like we speak of the enslaved in the abstract. We call them slaves, as if they are separate from their humanity, because that is the way they were treated," Townes said.

Townes submitted his DNA in a testing kit through Ancestry.com and learned he is 84% sub-Saharan African and 16% European. He never could conclusively identify which of Africa's 54 countries was his family's homeland, however.

"If you're European, you probably have documents to trace your ancestry back to your country of origin," he added. "For us, there's a disconnect because we got on the ships as cargo. We were only identified by gender and age."

Townes eventually was able to trace his ancestry to Amelia County, to a slaveowner named Thomas J. Townes.

In 1860, Thomas J. Townes owned 66 slaves and had a net worth of $65,000. By 1870, he had gone bankrupt in the aftermath of the Civil War and President Abraham Lincoln's Emancipation Proclamation.

"Such was the business of owning enslaved people, that men prospered on the backs of our ancestors who were bought and sold for the benefit of others," Townes said.

"That's part of my story, my personal search for my ancestors and the history of Bermuda Hundred."

The Chesterfield Historical Society of Virginia's African American History Committee, of which Townes has been a member for 13 years, has embarked on a project to formally recognize the Bermuda Hundred riverfront as the place where many enslaved African people landed in America.

There are plans to create an interpretive marker at First Baptist Church Bermuda Hundred, which long ago saw both enslaved Africans and slaveowners worshipping at the same service and still maintains an active African American congregation today.

"We have to honor our ancestors by marking the place where they first set foot in Virginia," Townes said. "It's an untold story of Chesterfield County history."

The visualizations of Rose Hill and our family tree are more than just diagrams. They are proof of a living legacy. Every home, every field, and every grave tells a story of survival, ingenuity, and determination.

Through them, the connection to Monticello is not abstract—it is tangible, alive, and threaded through my own life as a descendant of those who refused to be defined solely by the history of slavery.

Rose Hill represents what my ancestors built: a space where they could control their labor, educate their children, worship freely, and honor their dead.

It is the living counter-narrative to the Monticello estate, showing that while Jefferson's wealth and influence are recorded in history books, the true legacy lies in the communities his enslaved families created outside the gates.

Understanding this duality — Monticello's history and Rose Hill's legacy — provides the foundation for my journey of discovery and identity, a story I now carry forward for future generations.

The Monticello updated

Chapter Ten — Reclaiming A Place in History

By the end of the nineteenth century, long after the plantation system that had defined Virginia for generations began to collapse, African American families across the region were building something new.I

n the hills near Monticello, members of the Sampson family and others established the Rose Hill Community.

A surviving land deed records the foundation of what would become a self- sustaining settlement built by Black families determined to control their own land and future.

Rose Hill was more than a collection of houses. It was a functioning community.

There was a farm that provided work and food for residents. A church stood at the center of the settlement, serving as both a spiritual home and a meeting place for families whose lives had been shaped by generations of struggle.

The community also built a training school where young people learned practical trades alongside traditional education. Skills like farming, carpentry, and construction were passed down so the next generation could sustain the independence their parents had fought to achieve.

Homes spread across the land surrounding the church and school, forming a network of families who supported one another through work, worship, and shared purpose.

Even in death the community remained united. The Rose Hill cemetery became the resting place for generations of residents, including members of the Smith and Sampson families.

Among those buried there was my great-grandmother, Helen Louise Smith, whose life was part of the legacy of the Rose Hill settlement.

While the world remembers the grand estate on the nearby mountain, communities like Rose Hill tell another story — the story of African Americans who built their own institutions, their own landholdings, and their own future outside the gates of the plantation.

For many years, the story of Rose Hill and the Sampson family lived mainly within family gatherings and reunion conversations.

In 1994, at one of the early Sampson family reunions, relatives welcomed a younger family member who had come searching for answers about his heritage. That family member was Hugh Carter.

At the reunion, his aunts and other relatives presented him with a collection of family history documents and research that had been compiled over many years.

The package contained photographs, written recollections, and genealogical notes tracing the family's connection to Albemarle County and the Rose Hill community.

As the stories were shared, family members expressed a hope that someone would eventually write the full history of the Sampson family.
Hugh Carter told them that one day he would.

The research that followed revealed a deeper and more complex story than anyone had initially realized. It uncovered connections to slavery through the Coleman line and documented the remarkable achievements of Charles and Laura Sampson in building the Rose Hill farm.

As I began tracing my father's family line, the names revealed a clearer path into the past. My father, Hugh Harris, was the son of Joseph Henry Harris Sr., whose

father was Henry Clay Harris.

Through my father's mother, Rosa Smith Harris, the Harris family was connected to the Smith and Sampson families who helped build the Rose Hill community. That meant the story of Rose Hill was not a distant piece of history—it was part of my direct lineage.

My father's mother, Rosa Smith Harris, came from the Sampson-Smith families who founded the Rose Hill community in 1892. That settlement included a farm, a church, a cemetery, and a training school — institutions that ensured the community's independence and resilience after emancipation.

Grace Coleman married Henry Clay Harris, bringing together two generations that had endured the transition from slavery to freedom. Their son, Joseph Henry Harris Sr., carried the family forward, followed by my father, Hugh Harris, and ultimately me.

Tracing this lineage connects me directly to Rose Hill, a community built not just to survive, but to thrive. It also places my family in the historical orbit of Monticello, where my ancestors lived and labored, and where families like the Colemans and others formed their own legacies outside the gates of the plantation.

Generations before I was born, families like the Sampsons and Smiths had built farms, homes, a church, and a training school on that land. Their work created a community that would sustain their descendants long after the plantation era had ended.

More importantly, it showed how the family's journey reflected a broader American story — one that moved from slavery to land ownership, from exclusion to resilience.

Reclaiming a place in history is not only about correcting records. It is about honoring the lives and sacrifices of those who came before.

Through research, documentation, and storytelling, descendants ensure that the legacy of Rose Hill and the Sampson family will continue to be remembered.

History remembers the house.

But the real story of Monticello lies in the families who surrounded it.

For generations, the Coleman family maintained that their lineage was somehow connected to Thomas Jefferson.

Historians have acknowledged the existence of that oral tradition, though the full truth remains difficult to document.

What is certain is that Jefferson's world was deeply intertwined with other powerful Virginia families, including the Eppes family.

Through marriage and inheritance, Jefferson and the Eppes families shared land, property, and enslaved laborers. Estate records show that enslaved people moved between their plantations as part of inheritance settlements.

These transactions reveal how the wealth of Virginia's planter elite depended on the labor of enslaved

communities whose stories were rarely recorded.

Within those communities lived families like the Colemans.

Thomas Coleman lived and worked in the orbit of Monticello. Later, his wife Eliza Coleman would stand at the gate of Jefferson's estate, greeting visitors who came to see the house on the mountain.

For generations, the Coleman family maintained that their lineage was somehow connected to Thomas Jefferson.

Historians have acknowledged the existence of that oral tradition, though the full truth remains difficult to document.

What is certain is that Jefferson's world was deeply intertwined with other powerful Virginia families, including the Eppes family.

Through marriage and inheritance, Jefferson and the Eppes families shared land, property, and enslaved laborers. Estate records show that enslaved people moved between their plantations as part of inheritance settlements.

These transactions reveal how the wealth of Virginia's planter elite depended on the labor of enslaved communities whose stories were rarely recorded.

Within those communities lived families like the Colemans.

Thomas Coleman lived and worked in the orbit of Monticello. Later, his wife Eliza Coleman would stand at

the gate of Jefferson's estate, greeting visitors who came to see the house on the mountain.

Afterword — Standing at the Gate Today

Today, the physical gates that once marked the boundaries of farms and estates in Albemarle County may no longer hold the same power they once did.

But the symbolism remains.

Standing at the gate today means looking both backward and forward.

It means remembering the ancestors who endured slavery, poverty, and hardship while still building families and communities that survived for generations.

It also means recognizing the progress that has been made and the work that remains ahead.

The land at Rose Hill still holds meaning for the descendants of those who built it.

It is a reminder that history is not only written in monuments and archives but also in the lives of ordinary families who refused to give up hope.

The gates that once separated people can now serve as symbols of connection — linking the past to the present and guiding future generations toward a deeper understanding of their heritage.

Author's Note

This book represents years of family research, oral history, and personal reflection.

Much of the information contained in these pages comes from family members who preserved stories across generations, including those who organized the early Sampson family reunions and gathered historical documents.

Their dedication to preserving the family's past made this work possible.

Acknowledgements

The author gratefully acknowledges the Sampson, Coleman, and extended family members whose memories, records, and encouragement inspired this book.

Special appreciation goes to those who organized the Sampson family reunions and shared historical documents that helped reconstruct the family's story.

References & Historical Sources

Research for this book draws from:
• Albemarle County historical archives
• oral histories from Sampson family members • genealogical research and family records
• regional studies related to Monticello
• records connected to
Rose Hill Baptist Church
• education history from
Albemarle Training School

Eliza Coleman's former home today

Appendix A

The Daily Progress

turday   Charlottesville, Virginia   4.8.06   www.DailyProgress.com

Many mortgages about to

s rate caps expire, payments are going to jump

WASHINGTON POST NEWS SERVICE

First it was terrorism. Then ock market crash. Then rising energy prices.

Are you ready for the next tacle for consumers?

Millions of cheap, teaser-e mortgages that people t out a few years ago, when rest rates were rock-bottom are about to get much more expensive.

More than $1 trillion in mortgage debt costing only 4 percent or so — rates locked in three years ago — is about to soar in price to nearly 8 percent in some cases.

With consumers already stressed by credit card payments, high gas and electric prices and meager raises, economists worry that the mortgage changes will put a new crimp in retail spending.

"It just suggests that consumers, particularly lower-end consumers, are going to be more stretched when these loans reset, with potentially negative implications for spending growth," says Scott Hoyt, director of consumer economics at Moody's Economy.com.

For somebody with a $150,000 mortgage payable over 30 years, a pop from 4.5 percent to 7.5 percent would mean a payment increase from $760 to $1,050. That's nearly $300 removed from a household's free monthly cash flow, all at once.

This will happen because of a relatively new breed of loan — the hybrid adjustable mortgage. Traditional adjustable mortgages

See RATES on A9

Finding a past at Monticello

Paul C. Harris, the former delegate for the 58th District, filled the seat in the Virginia legislature once held by Thomas Jefferson. Now Harris has discovered that his family has deep roots at Jefferson's home.

Mou guide sugg

BY JESSI
Daily Progr

When the Moun Committee met last n an ordinance restri Albemarle County's complete.

But it's a lot easie general ideas in a craft final language group, and the differe ber committee emerg finalized on a docume ing.

"Everyone saw th nance that they beli member Jeff Werr Environmental Coun out in 'thou shalt n more complicated."

"""

Continued from A1

Harris and Coles accept the ties as far back as they are known with growing pride and curiosity.

"It's an incredible story," Harris said. "The important research conducted at Monticello confirms that my family is an important stitch in the American fabric. I am proud of my ancestors who helped grow, cultivate and preserve the Monticello that Americans know, love and cherish as their own."

Oral history catalogued

Stories that were handed down from one generation to the next are finding new historical context on Monticello's Web site, www.monticello.org, where Harris recently said he discovered photographs and discussion of his family.

The text describes his family as having worked at the gatehouse on Route 53 as gatekeepers. For the extended family, "Monticello was home for almost two centuries, much longer than for anyone who held title to the property."

"My jaw dropped" when he clicked on the Monticello's Gatekeepers page of an oral history section, Harris said. Up popped a photograph of his maternal grandparents, Joseph and Rosa Harris, and a 1912 photo of Eliza Coleman, his great-great grandmother, standing in front of the gatehouse. His grandfather "looked very proud, and he was very well-dressed. I just love that picture."

"Even today, our family are cooks

Joseph Harris, grandson of Eliza Coleman, and his wife, Rosa Harris, are Paul C. Harris' grandparents.

Mary Elizabeth Henderson, a distant relative of Harris, was the Monticello gatekeeper for almost 50 years.

[and caretakers] who pride themselves to be looking out for people," he said. "It's the mentality of a gatekeeper."

Coles, whose photo albums contain generations of ancestors at Jefferson's front gate a mile from where she and seven of her nine siblings were born, said family lore includes warm and vivid tales of playing around the gatehouse and on Monticello Mountain.

"We all used to go there because our aunt used to live up there at the gate. That was our playground all summer long," said Coles. "We always knew Thomas Jefferson was kin to us. We were always told that."

"We called Thomas Jefferson 'Uncle Thomas,'" out of affection and perhaps kinship, she said. In the family's oral history, "we were always told Sally Hemings was one of their relatives."

One of her photo albums contains a May 23, 1955, Daily Progress with a story about the previous day's fire that destroyed the home where she was born and killed three members of her family. In that article, Mrs. J.H. Morris of 501 Park St. is quoted as saying the burned-out family of Joseph and Rosa Harris "are direct descendants of slaves at Monticello."

Morris was collecting clothing for the family, said Coles, who was employed at the home of Morris, whose first name was Rachel. "Here's a white woman who knew our history, but we didn't know she knew."

Genealogy investigated

Stanton, the Shannon senior historian at Monticello, said that since 1993 the Thomas Jefferson Foundation has interviewed almost 170 descendants and others who believe they are connected to the Monticello of Jefferson's time, but we've been unable to pin it down or get further back than the 1800s."

"Nevertheless, the Colemans were longtime residents of Monticello in the period of Levy ownership [between 1834 and 1923] and their descendants have wonderful memories of visiting them at the Monticello gatehouse," Stanton said.

Monticello historians have been unable, so far, to establish a definite connection between Harris and slaves at Monticello owned by Jefferson, she said.

"We do know that Thomas and Eliza Coleman lived and worked at Monticello in the early years of the 20th century," Stanton said. "And it seems highly probable that Thomas Coleman was the son of a slave [of] Joel Wheeler, who was the caretaker of Monticello" from the period of the Civil War until 1878.

Hunting history

Sam Towler, who has written about Monticello residents from 1853 to 1863, said the Thomas Coleman who married Eliza appears to be a grandson of Thomas Coleman Sr., a slave belonging to Wheeler, who prior to 1860 was overseer at Carter's Bridge for Benjamin Franklin Randolph, a grandson of Thomas Jefferson.

Towler, a cousin of Wheeler's adopted son, said court records indicate that the man he believes to be a direct ancestor of Paul Harris' grandfather died at Monticello in 1888 at age 80 and could have lived there during the period before Jefferson died there on July 4, 1826.

"The Thomas Coleman born in 1808 ... must have lived on the grounds [of Monticello], and the Thomas Coleman born in 1830 also," said Towler, whose mother's family had lived at Monticello during the Civil War. "My best guess is that the gatehouse was built in the 1850s," he said.

Wiencek, who has written two books about slave families in the 1800s and researched the lives of Jefferson's slaves, said that family oral history is a "very tricky source."

But, Wiencek believes, some of Paul Harris' direct ancestors not only were slaves at Monticello in the 1860s but that the Colemans at the gatehouse had American Indian ancestry — an opinion shared by Coles, Harris' aunt.

"It's very plausible," said Wiencek, a member of the state Library Board.

"We were Cherokee Indians," Coles said matter-of-factly.

Monticello appears as glad to welcome Harris into the history of Jefferson's home as the former dele-

Above, the Monticello gatehouse was the home of former Del. Paul C. Harris' ancestors. Below, a photo from 1912 shows Harris' great-great grandmother Eliza Coleman in front of the gatehouse.

gate is to claim the ties.

"I talked to Paul and he is so excited about it," said Daniel P. Jordan, president of the Thomas Jefferson Foundation, owners of the presidential home since a 1923 purchase from the Levy family that held the property for 89 years.

"What could be more exciting than to discover that an ancestor was part of history in a conspicuous way," Jordan said.

"It's Monticello's goal to approach the past in the most accurate possible way, which means taking an inclusive approach," he said. "Jefferson is front and center, but hundreds of other individuals, including an enslaved community, are important parts of the story."

What goes around ...

Harris was elected to Jefferson's former seat in the House of Delegates in 1997 and re-elected in 1999. He was the first black Republican elected to the General Assembly in more than 100 years.

Harris resigned his seat in 2001 to work in the U.S. Justice Department. He is now senior counsel and director of enterprise compliance for Raytheon, a major U.S. defense contractor in Arlington.

He said he has not given up a desire to run for statewide office someday.

"My passion for politics still burns, but I am at a point where I would have to make a very sober decision about what to do," Harris said.

He said he and his family hope to learn more about the family's long ties to Monticello.

"It's been sort of like a history lesson and learning about the family," Harris said. "We just recently have started to have annual family reunions and that has rekindled interest as well. The younger generation has taken a real keen and active interest in family history."

Anyone might do the same if the family history referred to America's third president as "Uncle Thomas."

Contact Bob Gibson at (434) 978-7243 or bgibson@dailyprogress.com.

Vol. 221, No. 36   Published every Tuesday and Friday   Friday, May 5, 2006   609-924-

THE PRINCETON

Home assessments jump nearly 250 percer

By Emily Craighead
Staff Writer

WEST WINDSOR — The results of the township-wide property revaluation are in, and values increased nearly 2½ times since the last revaluation in

Individual homeowners are seeing a range of increases in their assessments, Tax Assessor Steve Benner said, with the average home assessment increasing from $239,500 in 2005 to $575,200 in 2006.

But not all homes have risen in value at the same rate as the average home, Mr. Benner pointed out.

"It depends on when they came into existence and how fast values have risen versus how fast values have risen in other parts of the town," he explained. "Market changes are not always uniform."

In Canal Pointe, for example, properties were assessed at about 30 percent of their true value before the revaluation — and have therefore risen more than 2½ times in value. But property assessments in Village Gran-

de were close
not change sig

"We need
as possible
this," Mr. Ber

As a resul
municipal ta
taxes, whose
sessed value
2006.

NSF funds major new engineering center at PU

By David Campbell
Staff Writer

The National Science Foundation has funded a multimillion-dollar engineering research center based at Princeton University that is expected to revolutionize sensor technology, the university's School of Engineering and Applied Science announced this week.

The goal of the research is to produce inexpensive and easy-to-use devices that will revolutionize such things as how doctors care for patients, agencies monitor air quality, and scientists study greenhouse gases in the atmosphere.

Princeton is partnering with the University of Maryland, Rice University, Johns Hopkins University, Texas A&M University and the City College of New York.

The Mid-Infrared Technologies for Health and the Environment, or MIRTHE center will combine the work of about 30 faculty members, 30 graduate students and 30 undergraduates from the six universities.

The center will collaborate with industrial partners to turn the technology into commercial products, and also will partner with groups in outreach that will seek to use MIRTHE's research as a vehicle for improving science and engineering education.

A 1928 photograph shows Rosa and Joseph Harris, Princeton resident Charles Phox's grandparents, with his aunt, Louise Harris. The Phox family believes the Harrises are descendents of Thomas Jefferson through a child he fathered with slave Sally Hemings.

Local family's roots gain

The Princeton Packet in Princeton, NJ

Roots

Continued from Page 1A

mother, Eliza Coleman — a gatekeeper at Jefferson's Monticello home believed to be related to Ms. Hemings within two generations, Mr. Phox said.

However, Eliza Coleman, whose maiden name is unknown by the family, is the oldest verifiable relative of the Phox family. The ancestry of Eliza's parents is the missing link of information sought by Mr. Phox's family to confirm to all what they — through spoken words — have known for years.

"What we've been trying to find out is (Eliza's) maiden name," Mr. Phox's aunt and unofficial family historian Sylvia Coles said. Ms. Coles, a resident of Charlottesville, Va. — located near Monticello — said the family has always had deep roots at the Jefferson estate and a verbal understanding of the magnitude of their connection. As a child, Ms. Coles recalls visiting the property with the wish of going to "Uncle Tom's" house.

But the discovery of the photographs — which proved that Mr. Phox's family is certainly connected with Monticello — in one way or another — was made quite by chance. While researching the president's estate on the Monticello Web site, Mr. Phox's first cousin, Paul Harris — coincidentally, a former Virginia state delegate who was elected in 1997 to the legislative seat once held by Jefferson — unearthed photographs of his relatives.

The photographs, found in "Getting Word," the Monticello African American oral history project featured online at www.monticello.org, include a 1912 photograph of Eliza Coleman in front of the gatehouse as well as a photograph of Mr. Phox's grandparents, Joseph and Rosa Harris. Joseph Harris — Ms. Coles' late father — was the grandson of Eliza Coleman.

Although historians have not officially recognized that Eliza Coleman was, in fact, related to Sally Hemings — historians as a whole haven't confirmed that the affair between the president and his slave mistress occurred — Mr. Phox said he has more than oral genealogical history to lead him to believe she was.

"Only so many people were given a good position at Monticello, and those people were descendents of Ms. Hemings," Mr. Phox said, adding that his great-great grandmother and her husband, Thomas, were gatekeepers at the estate who lived there for years.

Further, Mr. Phox said, the 500 acres owned by his family near Monticello is a sure sign that the connection to the third president exists.

Mr. Phox said the slaves with whom President Jefferson had a particular connection — namely Sally Hemings and her kin — were left a piece of property according to his will. "That is why my family has 500 acres," he said, adding the family is currently in a brainstorming phase to decide what to ultimately do with the property.

While Mr. Phox says the presidential connection has always been common knowledge in his family, the discovery of the photos was a satisfying revelation.

"We've always known for some years, but we never had actual proof," Mr. Phox said.

For now, family members say that they are enjoying the pursuit of more evidence to verify a family tree of such historical importance.

"We all get excited when we find out a little bit more," Ms. Coles said, adding that several members of her extended family ranging from New Jersey to Washington, D.C. and Charlottesville are involved in the research effort.

Ms. Coles said the family would love to have scientific proof through DNA studies that the connection exists — but mainly for posterity. "We grew up knowing enough, but if there is anything more it would help our grandchildren and children," she said. "It would be good for them to know."

Mr. Phox — equally confident in the authenticity of the family's oral history — said finding the visual proof of a Monticello connection has been gratifying for his family and has pushed him to continue the research

"It feels good because it makes you feel like you're part of American history, and that's actually what we are," he said.

Princeton Packet

Early Fire Claims Lives Of Three Simeon Children

FOUR OTHER OCCUPANTS ESCAPE — *1955*

Simeon, Va.—This Albemarle County community, just four miles southeast of Charlottesville, was t h e scene of a fire early last Sunday m o r n i n g that claimed the lives of three Negro children.

The hysterical cries of the children awakened the other four occupants, who hastily vacated the rapidly burning two story frame house.

Burned to death in the flaming home were Francis Harris, 10, daughter of Mrs. Rosa Harris; Deborah, 3, and Paulette Harris, 2, both grandchildren of Mrs. Harris.

Sylvia Harris, 17-year-old daughter of Mrs. Harris, jumped from a second floor window as the roof caved in. She suffered a broken foot and several fractured toes.

Mrs. Harris and her other two children also received injuries as they escaped from the fire. She was severely burned on her hands and side. Her daughter, Pauline Harris, 13, received burns on her hands and legs, and son, Hugh, 19, was burned on the hands and arms.

D e p u t y Sheriff T. M. Whitten said the survivors told him they were awakened by the screams of the three children who perished in an upstairs room but were unable to rescue them.

Charlottesville f i r e men responded quickly to the call but were unable to control the fire which was far advanced when they arrived. While the cause of the blaze was not determined immediately, Fire Chief Lionel Key ruled out faulty wiring as the cause following his examination of electrical circuits.

The four survivors were rushed to the University of Virginia Hospital shortly after their escape from the burning dwelling. Mrs. Harris and her daughter, Pauline are patients at the hospital where their condition is reported as being satisfactory. Hugh and Sylvia

My father Hugh Harris was 19 at the time. All of my family previous article 1955

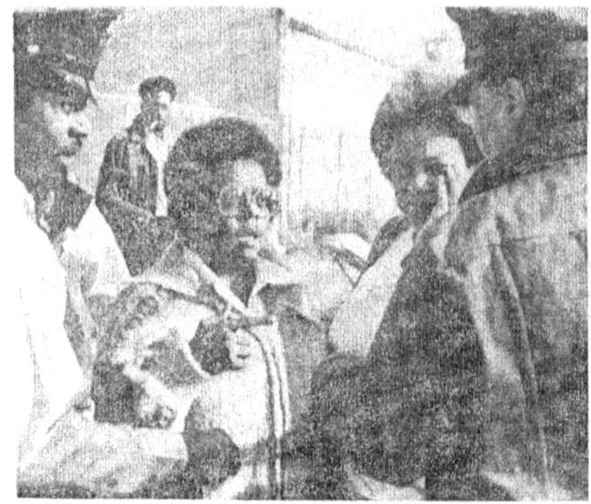

Boys Played With Matches Often Before Fatal Fire

By CHUCK DAVIS
Staff Writer

An early morning rowhouse fire that killed a 3-year-old Trenton boy and left his 2-year-old brother in guarded condition yesterday was apparently started by one of the children playing with matches, according to a fire official.

The blaze which ripped through the 2½-story frame home at Kelsey and Short Avenues in the West Ward "appeared to have been started when a match was dropped into a stuffed chair in the middle room of the first floor," said Battalion Chief Joeseph Stein.

Neighbors and relatives told the chief one of the children had a habit of playing with matches, Stein said.

Shawn Carter, 3, was pulled from the second floor of the burning building by fireman Blaine Shaddo, but life-saving efforts at the scene and in the hospital failed to revive him, officials said.

He was pronounced dead at 10:30 a.m. in Mercer Medical Center.

His brother, Aaron, 2, pulled from the flames by fireman Robert Ervin and rushed to Philadelphia's Children's Hospital by helicopter, was listed in guarded condition in an acute care unit, a hospital spokeswoman said.

Six other persons were in the home when the fire began, Stein said. Three were taken to the hospital and treated and released.

The children's mother, Wetonah, was at a nearby laundromat when the fire began, officials said.

Rosie Nollie, 20, visiting the Carter's with her two children, Nicki and Reinell, spotted the fire and escaped to the roof of the home. The two Carter children apparently did not follow Nollie, officials said.

More than 20 firemen from five city companies responded to the blaze at 9:05 a.m. and fought it for 40 minutes, Stein said.

The fire spread to the adjoining building, occupied by Mary Allen, but was stopped before it burned through the roof, Stein added.

The persons treated and released were identified as Thomas Carter, 18, Charles Harris, 20, Charles Phox, 20.

Trentonian Photo By STEVE MERVISH

TRAGIC FIRE — Wetonah Carter, mother of three-year-old Shawn who was killed in a fire early yesterday in their home in the West Ward, speaks with Trenton Police Sgt. Vander McFarland and a fire official when she learned of the fire. A neighbor looks on.

The Trentonian Newspaper from Trenton, NJ they did a terrible job with this article in 1980. They mistakenly identified my mother Alice Harris, the woman on the left as my sister Wetonah Carter. The other woman was my Aunt Estelle Phox. My cousin Charles Phox (Aunt Estelle's son) and I jumped from the second floor window as the house was burning beneath us. I got burned on my arm and hand from hand jumping off the ledge of the window, also singing my facial hair. The article mistakenly identified me Hugh Carter as Thomas Carter 18, also mistakenly identified my younger brother Kevin Brian Harris who was 17 at the time as Charles Harris 20. My sister Wetonah Carter's three year old son Shawn Carter died that day. My two year old nephew Aaron was airlifted to Children Hospital of Philadelphia. My father almost died in 1955 house fire in this book.

238

Today's Market

Three Perish

$50 Fine Ordered On Driving Count

Polio Program

1955 House fire. Mrs. J. H. Morris recognized my family as direct descendants of slaves she knew

Family Oral History
This is the oral history from my great great grandfather and great great grandmother verbatim.

"Charles and Laura Sampson, Papa and Mama Sampson

For the last few years our attention has been focused on our African Heritage. Who our descendants were, where they embarked and from where they came,

It would be great if we could distinguish the tribe and clan, of course, thought thinking positive, we know we have a long hard job of research ahead.

Thus far, we have found that Papa Sampson was born in Fluvanna County. We do not know of his parentage as of yet.

Mama Sampson's birth place we think was someplace in Albemarle County. Aunt Daisy Smith remembered her grandmother, Cornelia Sheppard (Mama Sampson's mother) who resided with Aunt Willie. We have not as yet found any record of her father.

Having gone that far, we have to now go back. We have members the family, who are researching, hoping to find the missing links.

There are many things about Mama and Papa you will realize as you watch the documentary.

They were a very secure, spirit filled couple, who raised their family to seek high ideals and moral values, that they were the pedestal of the community, that they were above the average, that they would accomplish anything they wanted with initiative and endeavor.

Papa and Mama's home was built on the highest hill in the Rose Hill community. They had the most land, the biggest house and biggest oak tree on their lawn. They had the largest farm of Albemarle County. People came from miles around to purchase animal, produce and other products for their livelihood. There was no poverty in Papa and Mama's family.

It would take a book to write about the good and bad times of Papa and Mama Sampson. Hopefully someone will one day attempt to capture the full meaning and value of being of Sampson Heritage and of the Rose Hill Community.

I told my family that I would write a book about our family reunion and research over thirty years ago. The time is right.

So far as we know, neither Papa nor Mama was born into slavery, this was in 1994. We found out otherwise after further research we were born into slavery via Grace Coleman Harris side of the family.

Our earliest recollections were of the Charles Sampson's family residing at Tufton at the time of the Macom's.

Originally, Tufton was owned by Martha Jefferson Randolph, whose property was given by her father, Thomas Jefferson. At hat time, most property in that area of Albemarle County was owned by Jefferson. Papa and Mama However, lived and worked there as tenant farmers or sharecroppers. They knew little or nothing of racism, as most of the farmers were there for the same reason, to purchase their own land and raise their families. These tenants were both black and white. They prayed together and got what little education they could together. Neither felt superior to the other.

When Papa and Mama accumulated enough money, they bought their property and began to clear the land and hued the trees to build their home. At that time, everyone jumped in to help each other raise the buildings.

We know some of their older children were born at Tufton. When Papa and Mama moved into their home, they bought with them a few head of cattle, chicken, pigs and seeds for planting crops. Their personal property grew as did their respect in the growing community."

Few people were left at the "old quarters' as the living place was called where the tenants lived. Most of the blacks began building their own homes at Rose Hill and a few whites continued to live and work therefor years after, in the old run down shacks. Papa bartered and traded to obtain mules and other farm equipment. He had the most beautiful surrey with the fringe that could be closed when the weather was bad, this was for Sundays or special occasions.

Everything they used and ate was grown on their property. Mama took care of the garden and the chickens.

Along with her, the children and other neighbors picked berries for jams, jellies and canning vegetables from the gardening fruits from the orchards. She made the clothing, bed sheets, spreads and quilts. They owned sewing machine, an organ, a victrola and had lights powered by a deco motor. Most of these things were luxuries to many people. Mama and the girls milked the cows and made butter and cheese.

Besides these many chores, Mama cooked (example: fried apples, sausage, sidemeat, batter bread, eggs) breakfast.

Dinner which was about two in the evening, consisted of gumbo or stew with several vegetables.

Meats that she might fix consisted of : pork, beef or wild game such as rabbit, squirrel, opossum, ground hog, and sometimes deer or raccoon, with hoe cakes, cornbread or hot rolls.

Supper was light, some kind of sweet pie or cake, fruit and usually some kind of bread with milk and butter. On Sunday, the midday meal was special as the preacher man and wife usually dined with them.

This usually consisted of fried chicken, ham.roast beef, corn pudding or corn on the cob, depending on the season.

Several green vegetables and several deserts, mashed potatoes or potato salad, hot rolls and chilled butter milk.

The midday meal during the week was huge, because they had to feed the men who worked for Papa and Mama in the fields. The women in the family were kept quite busy.No matter how tired Papa and Mama were at night, we had our prayer and Bible reading and singing. Papa played an accordion. Everyone said their good nights and were off to bed in anticipation another day.

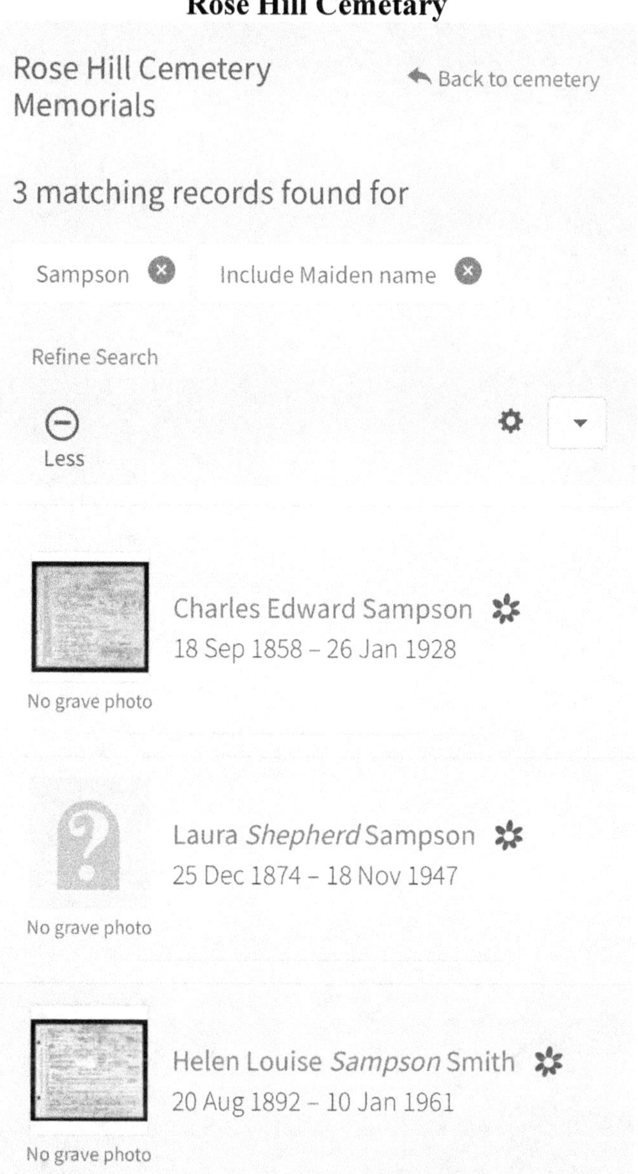

These family members are buried there today, on the right tombstone and marker Rose Hill

My great uncle Jacob Lee Sampson "Members of the family who once lived near Rose Hill would later serve the country in war, including a World War I veteran whose final resting place is now at Arlington National Cemetary on the left Rose Hill Cemetary tombstone and marker

Rose Hill Plat Map

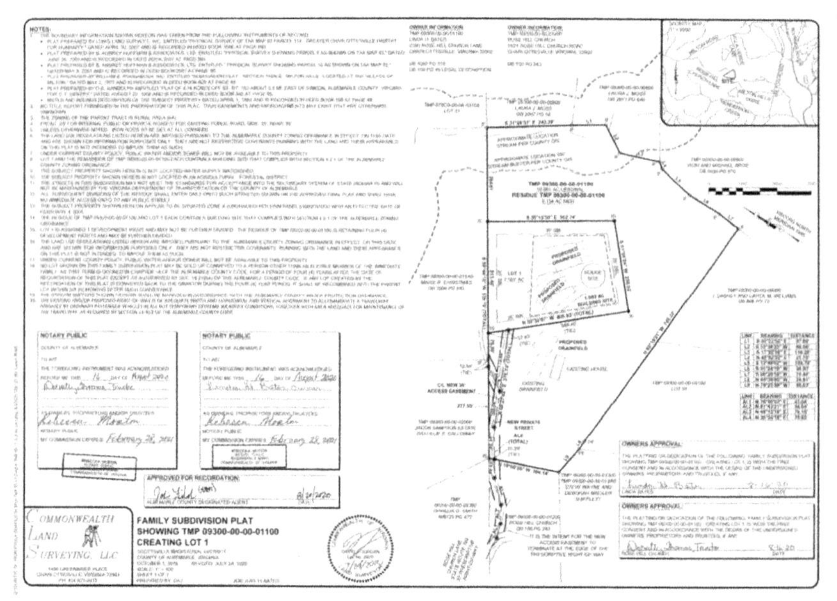

Rose Hil

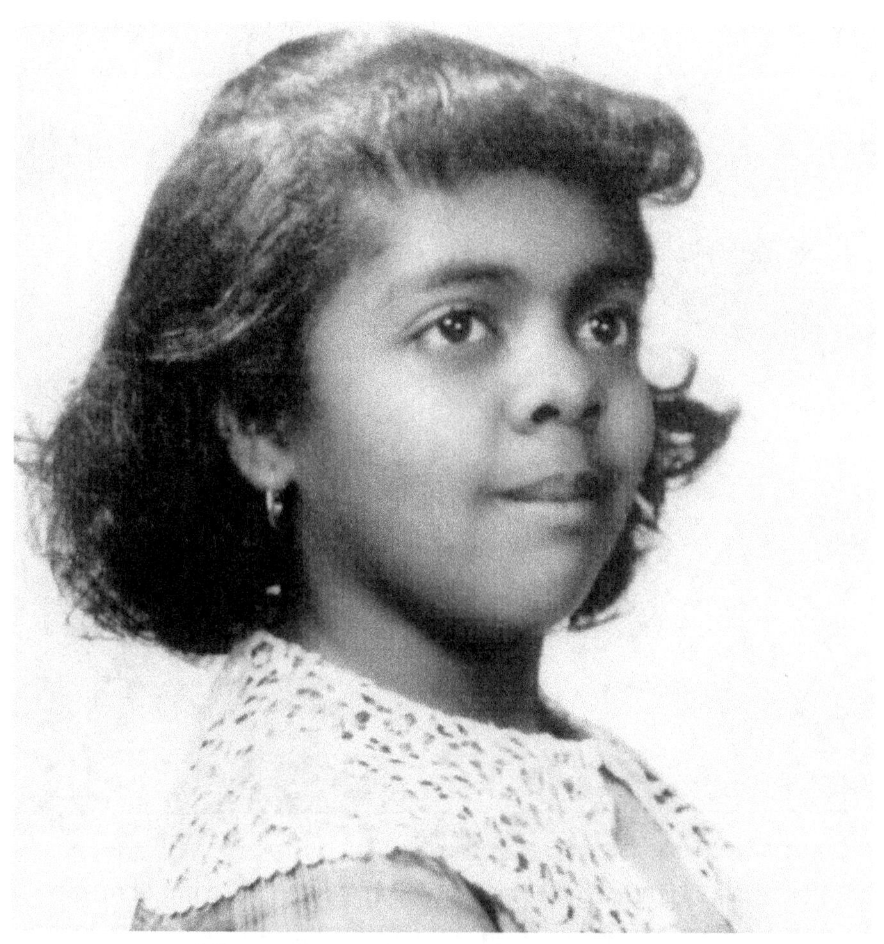

My mother Alice Harris . Thank you!

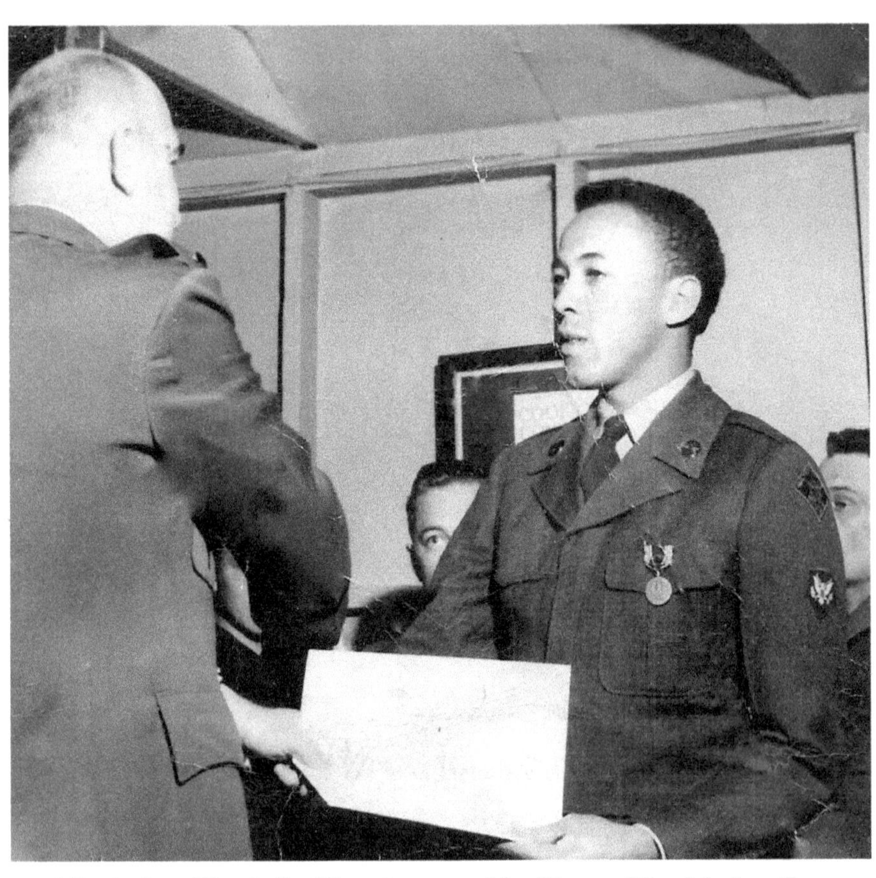

My father Hugh L. Harris served in Korea like his brother Joseph Harris Jr. who also served in Vietnam did 24 years in The Army. Thank you!

The Spirit Of My Ancestors

Army 41C MOS Training School

Thanks pop for planting that seed

I'm forever grateful

Me against the world

Me, my sister Wetonah Carter, her children and grandchildren

My mother, brother, nieces and nephews

My brother Kevin Brian Harris and my mother Alice Harris

Nieces and Nephews

Aunt Estelle, daughter Lisa and her grandson Michael Harris

Me with Professional fighter Olympic Gold Medalists Howard Davis.

First cousin Bee Phox (Barry Phox)

Nephews

Aunt Sylvia and me Harris Family Reunion 2022

Gov. Youngkin Appoints Four New UVA Board of Visitors Members

By Bethanie Glover, ffu4bm@virginia.edu
June 28, 2023

Virginia Gov. Glenn Youngkin appointed, from left, Paul C. Harris, Paul B. Manning, John L. Nau III and Rachel Sheridan to the UVA Board of Visitors on Wednesday. (Contributed photos)

irginia Gov. Glenn Youngkin on

Congratulations cousin Paul

2Souljiers with The Eloheem Team
Bee Phox single

Our first podcast

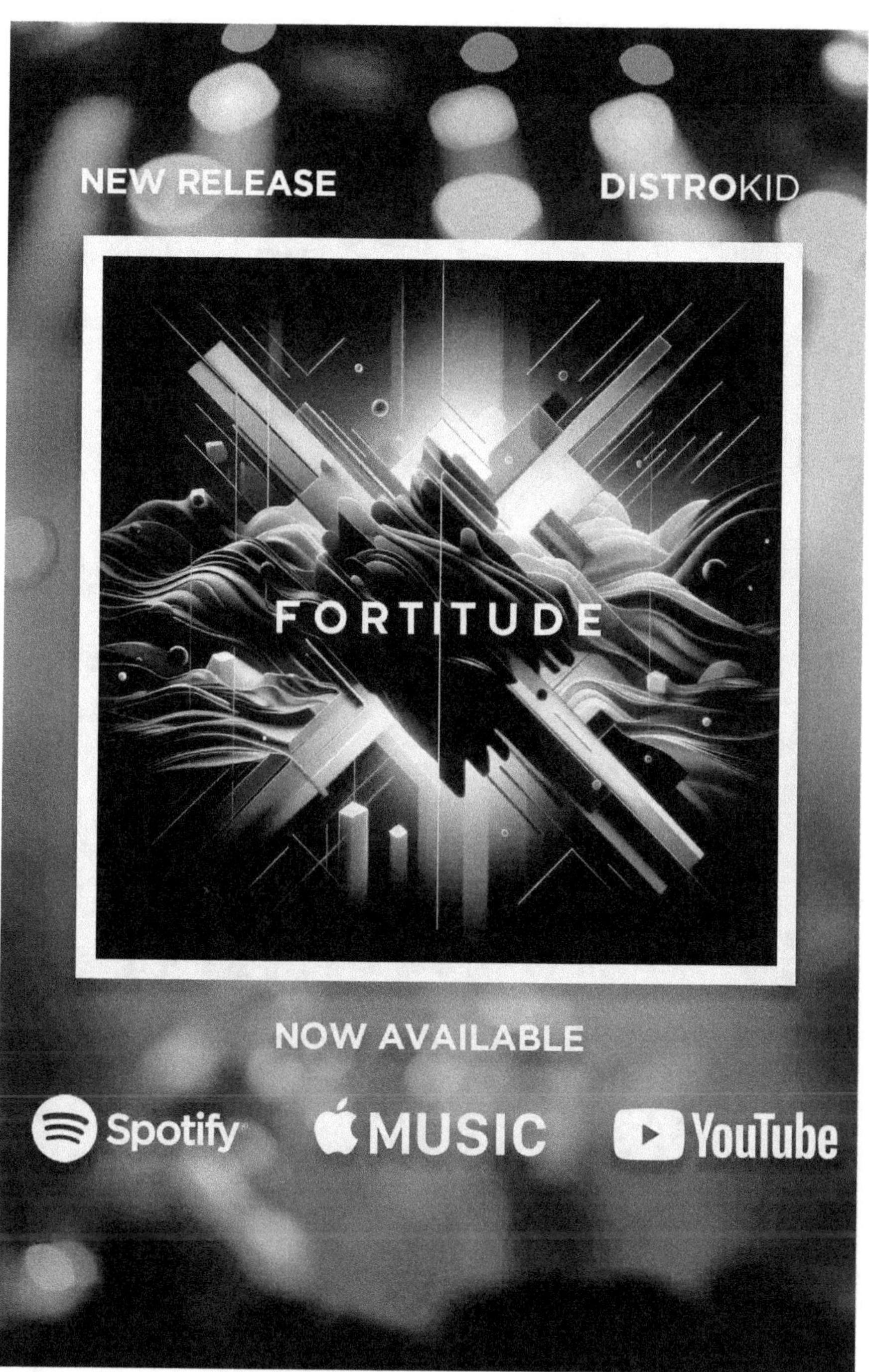

My first single Fortitude 2026 out now

My remix Fortitude R & B single version 2026 out now

Looking forward to what the future holds

☑ **Source Note / Disclaimer Page**

Unless otherwise noted, documents and images reproduced in this volume are drawn from the author's family collection. Where institutional records are incomplete or silent, family- held materials provide essential historical context.